FOREWORD

This book addresses unit 3.1 The Christian Church through a Study of the Catholic Church and One Protestant Tradition; and unit 3.2 The Christian Church with a Focus on EITHER the Catholic Church OR the Protestant Tradition.

As these units overlap but do not cover all of the same material you will find a separate contents page for each unit of study. Unit 3.2 is divided into two: 3.2a The Christian Church with a Focus on the Catholic Church and 3.2b The Christian Church with a Focus on the Protestant Tradition.

To follow your chosen unit of study you simply need to select the contents page that addresses your unit.

Each unit is labeled with a coloured button:

⬤ for unit **3.1 The Christian Church through a Study of the Catholic Church and one Protestant Tradition**

⬤ for unit **3.2a The Christian Church with a Focus on the Catholic Church**

⬤ for unit **3.2b The Christian Church with a Focus on the Protestant Tradition**

You will find buttons beside each section heading to indicate whether it is relevant to your chosen study or not. There are also handy Teacher's Notes to assist you further throughout the book. Remember you should always refer to CCEA's official specification and website (http://www.ccea.org.uk) for the most up-to-date information on your unit of study.

 For your folder  In a Group   Further Thinking

UNIT 3.1 THE CHRISTIAN CHURCH THROUGH A STUDY OF THE CATHOLIC CHURCH AND ONE PROTESTANT TRADITION

UNIT 3.2a THE CHRISTIAN CHURCH WITH A FOCUS ON THE CATHOLIC CHURCH

CHAPTER 6 SACRAMENTS AND ORDINANCES 95

CHAPTER 7 THE ROLE OF THE CHURCH IN CONTEMPORARY SOCIETY 129

UNIT 3.2b THE CHRISTIAN CHURCH WITH A FOCUS ON THE PROTESTANT TRADITION

Chapter 1

THE BIRTH, DEVELOPMENT AND BELIEFS OF THE CHURCH

THE EVENTS AND MEANING OF PENTECOST   ACTS 2: 1–8

The story of Pentecost is told in the Acts of the Apostles. This book follows immediately after the Gospels in the New Testament. Acts tells the story of the beginning of the Christian Church. It was written by Luke, the Gospel writer.

Jesus was crucified outside Jerusalem at the time of the Jewish Passover feast. After his Resurrection he told his disciples to wait in Jerusalem for the gift of the Holy Spirit. Luke tells us that the disciples were all gathered in the upper room of a house in Jerusalem on the Day of Pentecost, also called the Feast of Weeks. This is a Jewish harvest festival and a celebration of the giving of the Law of Moses. The word Pentecost means 'fiftieth' and it falls fifty days after Passover.

While the believers were in the upper room a noise like a strong wind suddenly filled the whole house. Then what seemed to be tongues of fire appeared and rested on each person. Everyone was filled with the Holy Spirit and began to speak in other languages.

'Descent of the Spirit', an engraving by Gustave Doré

IN A GROUP

1. What images or symbols are used in the account of Pentecost to show the presence of God?

2. Do you think there are any similarities between the nature of wind and fire and the nature of God?

WHAT HAPPENED NEXT?

Many pilgrims had gathered in Jerusalem to celebrate Pentecost. Jews from far and wide were packed into the streets on this special day. The Temple was central to their faith and it was important for them to offer a sacrifice to God there. At about nine o'clock in the morning, Jesus' disciples appeared in the streets. They were excited about something and a large crowd gathered to see what was going on. Peter, one of the disciples, began to preach to those gathered and claimed that Jesus of Nazareth was the promised Messiah. He called on the people to repent and be baptised and receive the gift of the Holy Spirit.

At the end of the day about 3,000 people had responded to Peter's message and were baptised, becoming the first members of the Christian Church. Pentecost is often referred to as the birthday of the Church.

ST PAUL'S TEACHING ON THE CHURCH

Statue of Paul in the Vatican

Paul was a Jewish convert to Christianity who travelled Europe and Asia spreading the news about Jesus and gathering new believers to set up churches. Much of the book of Acts is taken up with his work. When Paul was on one of his missionary journeys he set up a church in a place called Corinth. Paul kept in touch with the Christians in Corinth and other churches by writing letters.

SPIRITUAL GIFTS
1 CORINTHIANS 12:1–11

In the book of Corinthians Paul writes about **spiritual gifts** –special abilities given to believers by the Holy Spirit after Pentecost. These gifts are given *"for the common good"* (1 Corinthians 12:7), in other words, to benefit everyone.

Verses 8–10 list some of the gifts:

GIFTS OF THE HOLY SPIRIT	
Wisdom	A special understanding – seeing things from God's perspective.
Knowledge	A special insight into someone's life or a situation.
Faith	The ability to trust God.
Healing	Being able to miraculously cure someone from illness.
Miraculous powers	
Prophecy	Prophets in the Old Testament spoke God's words, often giving instructions or directions. This continued in the New Testament.
Ability to distinguish between spirits	Knowing if a spirit is from God or from the devil.
Ability to speak in different kinds of tongues	This refers to glossolalia – the ability to speak in an unintelligible heavenly language.
Ability to interpret tongues	This is the gift that makes sense of the gift of tongues. It means being able to explain the meaning of a message spoken in tongues.

Speaking in Tongues

'Speaking in Tongues' or glossolalia, is a spiritual gift where the Holy Spirit enables someone to speak in an unknown language. It is used for worship, and is still common in some churches today (see page 43).

It seems that there was some division and jealousy in the Corinthian church to which Paul was writing. He assures them that all the different spiritual gifts are from the same God, and all of the gifts together work for the good of the Church. Nobody is better than anyone else because of such gifts.

IN A GROUP

1. Read verses 1 Corinthians 12: 8–10 and make a list of the various gifts.

2. Do you think churches today should disagree about people's gifts?

FURTHER THINKING

Invite someone from a Pentecostal church to your school to talk about speaking in tongues.

THE CHURCH AS A BODY

1 CORINTHIANS 12:14–22, 25–27

The Church is really the people rather than the building where Christians meet. In the New Testament there were no church buildings such as we have today, so when the word 'church' is used in the Bible it always refers to people. Paul described the Church using the image of a 'body' (1 Corinthians 12:14–22). The church is made up of individual people who, like different parts of the human body, each have a different purpose. The different parts need to work together for the body to function properly. No part can be regarded as unnecessary or less important than another. The Church is made up of people with a variety of gifts and abilities (12:28). Every member of the Church is needed so no one should feel inferior (12:15–17).

Some ways that people make up the body of the Church are suggested in the following diagram:

Some are gifted leaders. This can mean giving wise advice, or deciding what direction the church should go.

Some people have the gift of preaching or teaching. This can mean taking small Bible studies or speaking to large groups.

Some may have a talent for putting together resources for the church to use. Others can think through problems facing the church and come up with answers.

Some people are good listeners. They can tell when someone is feeling depressed or worried and can go out of their way to be there for that person.

Practical work is important for all churches. Cleaning, moving chairs, driving the church bus, flower arranging, and even ringing the church bells.

Some are gifted as visitors of the sick and elderly.

Some travel abroad as missionaries.

Some are gifted at playing instruments and leading people in worship.

FOR YOUR FOLDER

Read 1 Corinthians 12:12–26

1. How does Paul compare the Church to a body? (v12–13)

2. Which body parts does Paul talk about to explain the importance of all the body parts?

3. What does Paul say happens if part of the body suffers?

4. Explain how this teaching is relevant to the Christian Church.

THE CHARACTERISTICS OF THE EARLY CHURCH

In its earliest days the Church didn't see itself as a new religion. They were followers of Jesus, mostly Jewish, who tried to live their lives the way Jesus had done, praying and helping others. After Pentecost the believers were filled with the Holy Spirit and began to spread the teachings of Jesus in Jerusalem. The ministry of early Church was exciting work to be involved in.

Authority given by Jesus

MATTHEW 10:1, 5–14

When Jesus was with the disciples, he had given them power and authority to carry on his work. In Matthew's Gospel we read how Jesus called his twelve disciples together and gave them authority to drive out evil spirits and to heal every disease and every sickness (Matthew 10:1, 5–14).

It was important for the disciples to be totally dependent on God for everything that they needed for their mission. They were given these instructions by Jesus:

- To give without being paid.
- Not to carry any money with them.
- Not to beg.
- Not to take an extra shirt or shoes or a walking stick with them.
- When they came to a town or village, to look for someone who was willing to welcome them and let them stay.
- If they were not made welcome in a home or town, to leave that place and shake the dust off their feet.

IN A GROUP

1. Why do you think most Christians today don't follow these instructions?
2. What can Christians today learn from the attitude of Jesus and the disciples?

Community

ACTS 2: 42–47

The first believers met together in their homes, eating and praying and praising God together. They shared everything they had and sold their possessions, giving to those who were in need.

Miracles

We also see in Acts that Jesus' power to perform miracles passed to the disciples. Jesus had given them the authority to heal and drive out evil spirits. That work continued. The book of Acts records many miracles performed by the disciples in the name of Jesus.

Prayer

We read in Acts that the followers of Jesus devoted themselves to prayer. It was when they were praying together constantly that the Holy Spirit came at Pentecost.

Breaking Bread

1 CORINTHIANS 11:23–25

Part of the worship of the early Church was remembering the last meal Jesus had with his disciples. We find evidence of this in the Acts of the Apostles and in Paul's letters in the New Testament. Paul stressed the importance of remembering this event in his first Letter to the Corinthians:

> *"For I received from the Lord the teaching that I passed on to you: that the Lord Jesus, on the night he was betrayed, took a piece of bread, gave thanks to God, broke it, and said, 'This is my body, which is for you. Do this in memory of me.' In the same way, after the supper he took the cup and said, 'This cup is God's new covenant, sealed with my blood. Whenever you drink it, do so in memory of me.'"*
>
> 1 Corinthians 11: 23–25

'The Last Supper' by Leonardo da Vinci

Serving Others
JAMES 2: 14–17

The importance of sharing continued as the Church grew. The letter of James is a collection of practical instructions written to 'all God's people scattered over the whole world.' In this letter James reminds the believers of the importance of giving to the needy:

> "My friends, what good is it for one of you to say that you have faith if your actions do not prove it? Can that faith save you? Suppose there are brothers or sisters who need clothes and don't have enough to eat. What good is there in your saying to them, 'God bless you! Keep warm and eat well!' if you don't give them the necessities of life? So it is with faith: if it is alone and includes no actions, then it is dead."
>
> JAMES 2: 14–17

Christian Behaviour
COLOSSIANS 3: 12–17

As well as teaching what the characteristics of the whole Church should be, Paul teaches about the behaviour of individual followers of Jesus in his letter to the Colossians. He instructed that they should be compassionate, kind, and patient, forgiving those who wrong them.

IN A GROUP

Qualities of a Christian:

compassion   kindness   gentleness
        patience   humility

Explain the meaning of these qualities. Do you think it is difficult for a person to have such qualities?

How can Christians today show each of them in their daily lives?

Hymn-singing

Singing was an important part of early Christian worship. Paul told the early believers to sing psalms, hymns, and sacred songs and to sing to God with thanksgiving in their hearts (Colossians 3:16).

Preaching and Teaching

Preaching is the word used for spreading or explaining the Gospel. It describes how Jesus' followers tried to tell others about the Kingdom of God. The Book of Acts explains how Paul preached to the Jews and Gentiles to try to convince them to become followers of Christ.

Teaching is different to preaching. Preaching was used to reach the unconverted and teaching was used for those who had become Christians. The disciples taught their converts about how to live their new lives as followers of Jesus.

FURTHER THINKING

Find out how preaching and teaching is carried out in churches today. You could use the internet to search a church's website. Make a list of events that take place throughout the week.

Characteristics of the early Church

a statement of the teachings of the Apostles. Some believe that it was actually put together by them, although perhaps not written down until later. From its earliest use there had been a tradition of memorising the Creed, rather than just reading it. It is used quite widely in acts of worship in a number of Christian denominations including Catholic, Lutheran, Anglican, Presbyterian and Methodist.

The Apostle's Creed
I believe in God, the Father Almighty
maker of heaven and earth
and in Jesus Christ His only Son our Lord,
who was conceived by the power of the Holy Spirit and
born of the Virgin Mary,
suffered under Pontius Pilate
was crucified, died and was buried
He descended into hell;
The third day He rose again from the dead,
He ascended into heaven
and sits at the right hand of God
the Father Almighty;
from whom He shall come to judge the living and the dead.
I believe in the Holy Spirit;
the holy catholic church;
the communion of saints;
the forgiveness of sins
the Resurrection of the body
and the life everlasting.
Amen.

FOR YOUR FOLDER

1. Read Acts 2:42, 44–47 and make a list of different characteristics of the early Church from these verses.
2. Which characteristics of the early Church can be found in churches today?
3. Explain what Paul taught about spiritual gifts in the church.
4. Describe how the message of the Gospel was spread by the early Christians.

THE APOSTLES' CREED AS A SUMMARY OF CHRISTIAN BELIEF, TRUTH AND MEANING

A **Creed** is a statement of belief or set of beliefs. The Apostles' Creed is a statement explaining the basic and central faith or beliefs of Christians. The Apostles Creed is so called because, according to the earliest tradition of the Christian Church, it is

IN A GROUP

Read the Creed above carefully. Identify as many statements of belief as you can. You should be able to find statements of belief about God, Jesus, the Holy Spirit and the Church. Compare notes with the group beside you.

Beliefs about God

The Creed expresses Christian belief that:

- God is the Creator of all things;
- God is Father, not only of Jesus, but of all people;
- God is almighty and all-powerful.

Beliefs about Jesus

The Creed also professes Christian belief in the **Incarnation**. This is the idea of God coming to earth and taking on human form as a man. *Incarnation* literally means 'becoming flesh'.

Christians believe that Jesus was both fully human and fully divine: Fully human because he was born as a human being; fully divine because he was supernaturally conceived by the Holy Spirit. His mother Mary was a virgin. Matthew and Luke's Gospel both emphasise the fact that Jesus was born of the Virgin Mary:

"Now all this happened in order to make what the Lord had said through the prophet come true, 'A virgin will become pregnant and have a son, and he will be called Immanuel' (which means 'God is with us.')" (Matthew 1:22–24)

"Mary said to the Angel "I am a virgin. How, then, can this be?" (Luke 1:34)

'The Annunciation', El Greco

> ### Did you know?
>
> Christians believe different things about the virginity of Mary. The Catholic Church teaches that Mary's virginity marks her as special. Not only was she a virgin when Jesus was born, but she remained a virgin for the rest of her life.
>
> Protestant denominations teach that Mary was a virgin when Jesus was born, but she did not necessarily remain a virgin, and would have had a family with Joseph.
>
> Some believe that the Gospels are emphasising that Jesus was special, and the 'Son of God', but he was actually born and conceived in the natural way.

Beliefs about the Crucifixion, Resurrection and Ascension

From the very earliest years of the Christian church, the death of Jesus was considered to be the most important aspect of his mission. By his death he paid for the world's sin and brought God's forgiveness.

It is not only Jesus' death that is important to Christians. Belief in Jesus' Resurrection and Ascension is the basis of the whole Christian faith:

- It proves that Jesus really was the Son of God and not just a good man.

- Jesus overcame the power of death. Christians hope for the same Resurrection.

- Christians believe that Jesus is alive. He lives supernaturally in the hearts of believers, and his teachings are lived out by his followers.

Christians differ in their understanding of the Resurrection of Jesus. Though many believe in a literal Resurrection, there is a range of views held within the Christian Church.

> *Jesus' Resurrection happened just as it says in the Scripture. It was a Resurrection of his body, not just his Spirit.*

> *Jesus did physically rise from the dead but he looked different. The Resurrection was a new and different form of life. When he appeared to his followers they sometimes didn't recognise him.*

> *Jesus' didn't physically rise from the dead. The Resurrection is a symbol of how Jesus lived on in the teaching and actions of his followers.*

CLASS DEBATE

Organise a class debate reflecting different Christian views on the Resurrection.

FOR YOUR FOLDER

Explain in your own words why the Resurrection of Jesus is the basis of the Christian faith.

Beliefs about Judgement

The Apostle's Creed expresses the belief that Jesus will be the judge of the living and the dead. This puts Jesus firmly and completely into the role of God.

Beliefs about the Holy Spirit

After Jesus had ascended into heaven, he sent the Holy Spirit to his followers as he had promised. The Holy Spirit came on Pentecost and strengthened the faith of the Apostles and gave them God's power. Christians believe that the Holy Spirit does the same today.

The Trinity

As well as teaching and professing what Christians believe about God the Father, Son and Holy Spirit, the Apostles' Creed also outlines the Christian belief in the Trinity: that, although there is only one God, he can be known as three persons: God the Father, God the Son and God the Holy Spirit.

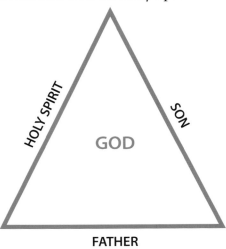

REMEMBER: Christians do not believe in **three** gods. They believe in **one** God who exists in **three** persons; in the same way that **one** triangle has **three** sides. Remove one side and you no longer have a triangle.

Beliefs about the Holy Catholic Church

In this context, the word 'church' refers to the people of God. The word 'catholic' means universal. So this statement is really declaring that the Christian Church is a world-wide fellowship of people who believe in and follow Christ.

Belief about the Communion of Saints

The word 'saint' appears a number of times in the New Testament and refers to those who believe in and follow Christ. So this is really a statement of the fellowship of all followers of Christ, both living and dead.

Belief in the forgiveness of sins, the Resurrection of the body and everlasting life

This expresses the Christian belief that all who believe that Christ died for the forgiveness of their sins and repent will have their sins forgiven. Christians also believe that as Jesus physically rose from the dead, they too will be with God forever after death.

FOR YOUR FOLDER

1. Explain, with examples from the creed, three main beliefs of the Christian Church.

2. What is meant by the term 'communion of saints'?

3. Explain what Christians understand by the term 'Holy Catholic Church'?

4. Explain the beliefs about judgement that are expressed in the Apostles' Creed.

IN A GROUP

"A true Christian must accept without question all the beliefs outlined in the Apostles' Creed. There is no room for difference of interpretation or opinion." Do you agree or disagree? Give reasons for your answer.

HOW CHRISTIANITY CAME TO IRELAND, THROUGH A STUDY OF THE LIFE AND WORK OF ST PATRICK

St Patrick is credited with 'bringing Christianity to Ireland' and is remembered as Ireland's patron saint. There are many myths and legends surrounding Patrick, but there are a number of reliable historical sources that allow us to chart how Christianity came to Ireland.

Christianity in Ireland before Patrick

There is strong evidence to suggest that there were already Christians in Ireland before the arrival of Patrick in the early to mid fifth century. Some of this evidence is as follows:

- There were some words used in the early Irish language which described Christian practices; for example, they had words for Easter, priest, Christian and church in their language.

- There is strong evidence that another bishop, named Palladius, was sent to Ireland before Patrick.

"Palladius, having been ordained by Pope Celestine, is sent as first bishop to the Irish believing in Christ" (Chronicle of Prosper of Aquitaine, AD431).

- Some traditions hold that there were four other missionaries in Ireland before Patrick: St Ciaran, St Declan, St Ailbe and St Ibar.

Many historians believe that these Christians first came to Ireland because of the contact Ireland had with the Christian Roman Empire through trade and travel and even from slaves captured by the Irish from Britain.

The *Confession* and *Letter to Coroticus*

Although there are many stories and legends about Patrick, the main historical sources are two documents that Patrick himself wrote.

The *Confession* was written almost as a spiritual diary. It tells us about his relationship with God and his calling and mission to the Irish, including its successes, dangers and difficulties. It is not really an autobiography because it leaves out many of the historical facts of his life, but it is the personal story of Patrick.

The *Letter to Coroticus* is a very different document. It was written to a prince called Coroticus who had carried out a raid on one of Patrick's Christian communities in Ireland. He had stolen many of their belongings and killed many of the Christians who had just been newly baptised. Those who were not killed were taken captive and sold as slaves. Patrick is angry and brokenhearted in his letter. He is personally hurt by this attack because it has been carried out by his fellow British countrymen who call themselves Christians and also because of his great love for his Irish converts.

The challenge of Paganism

From a study of Patrick's writings it is clear that the people he lived and worked among were pagan. They believed in many different gods such as Dagda and Lug and goddesses such as Brigit, Anu and Dana. The Irish considered wells and rivers, burial places and woodlands to be sacred places and often worshipped there. They also worshipped the sun. The Irish had many pagan feasts and festivals such as Imbolc and Lughnasa and had their own pagan priests called druids. These were very powerful in Irish society and would have been greatly opposed to the work of Patrick. Patrick disliked the pagan practices and wrote that the Irish worshipped "idols and unclean things".

> **Did you know?**
>
> The monument at Newgrange in County Meath might well have been used for the practice of sun worship by the Irish before the time of Patrick. It is one of the finest monuments to Ireland's pagan heritage.

A slave boy

Patrick was first brought to Ireland as a slave. At sixteen years old he was captured in a raid, taken from his father's villa in Britain to tend flocks on a mountainside in Ireland. He had no rights or status, no protection under law and he could not speak the language. He tells us that he had not been particularly religious, but at this time he came to know God and prayed "up to a hundred times a day and as many at night". After six years he escaped.

> **IN A GROUP**
>
> 1. For many years, a large proportion of the population of island of Ireland has considered itself Christian. Some argue that Ireland is now returning to Paganism in a new way. What do you think this means? Do you agree or disagree?

IN A GROUP

2. Patrick was taken to Ireland as a slave around the age you are now. How do you think he must have felt? Imagine you are the sixteen year old Patrick. Write a diary entry describing your thoughts and feelings as you spend your first night on a mountainside in Ireland.

A call to return

At home with his family once more, he had a dream. In the dream a man brought him many letters. As he read one entitled 'The Voice of the Irish', he heard them calling him: "We ask you holy boy to come and walk once more among us". Patrick had good reason never to return to the people who had enslaved him. He tells us that his family "begged me that I should never leave them, especially in view of all the hardships I had endured". However, he did indeed respond to their call.

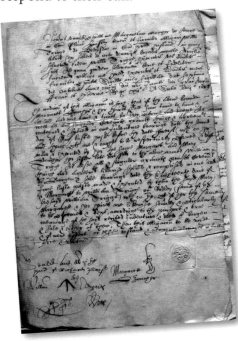

A difficult and dangerous mission

The clergy of his own church in Britain did not think Patrick suitable for the task. His education had been interrupted at sixteen when he was taken captive, so it seems they believed he was neither well enough qualified nor educated for such a mission. Patrick himself felt that his poor education made him unworthy to be bishop to the Irish, but in the end he was trained and sent to Ireland as bishop.

He tells us that his work was dangerous. Twelve times his life was in danger; he experienced many "traps and things which I cannot put into words". He tells us: "I daily expect to be murdered, robbed or reduced to slavery in one way or another" and "on one occasion they abducted my companions and me, and were frantically bent on killing me that day."

One of the worst moments of his mission was when a Welsh prince, Coroticus, launched raids in Ireland, killing and capturing many of Patrick's converts. Patrick also tells us that he longed to return home to see his relatives and friends: "How dearly I would love to go … God knows how much I yearned for it but I am tied by the Spirit … and I am afraid of undoing the work which I have begun … Christ the Lord has commanded me to come here and stay with them for the rest of my life."

IN A GROUP

1. Patrick could be described as a 'missionary' to Ireland. Use the internet or a library to find out about the experiences of missionaries today.

2. How does the experience of Patrick in Ireland compare with the experiences of missionaries today?

A successful mission

Patrick tells us in his confession that in spite of all the difficulties he "baptised many thousands". "The number of converts cannot be counted". He ordained priests and many became "monks and virgins for Christ".

He converted the Irish by preaching the Gospel to them and administering the three sacraments of Initiation: Baptism, Eucharist and Confirmation.

Despite often longing to return home, Patrick knew he could never leave his beloved converts. He remained in Ireland until death, prepared even to die for his converts if that is what God expected of him: "I gave up my free born status for the good of others. Should I be worthy I am ready to give even my life, promptly and gladly; and it is here that I wish to spend it until I die, if the Lord should grant it to me."

The Teachings of Patrick

Here are some of Patrick's teachings.

- The goal of the Christian is to always try to do better so that they can be perfect: "Would that you too, reach out to greater things and do better. This will be my happiness, because a wise son is the glory of his father."

- The Gospel should be the main motive behind all that the Christian does: "I never had any motive other than the Gospel and its promises to go back to that nation which previously I had only barely escaped".

- Christians should speak out against injustice: "compelled by concern for God and the truth of Christ and out of love for neighbour."

- Those who steal and murder put themselves outside the Church: "They will be slaves of hell in everlasting punishment ... they are estranged from me and Christ my God."

- Christians who associate with those who do grave wrongs are also guilty: "It is not permitted to court the favour of such people, to take food or drink with them, or even to accept their alms … which of the faithful would not shrink in horror from making merry or enjoying a meal with people of this sort? They have filled their houses with the spoils of dead Christians, they make their living on plunder."

- All Christians should be united because they share one baptism. He asks Coroticus and his men: "perhaps we do not belong to the same fold and do not have the same God as Father? … Perhaps they do not believe that we have received one and the same baptism or that we have one and the same God as Father?"

- Greed is a sin and is at the root of so many other sins. In particular it is wrong to gather wealth and riches at the expense of others or to benefit from the misfortune of others: "offering sacrifice from the property of the poor is just as evil as slaughtering a son in the presence of the father. The riches which he has gathered unjustly shall be vomited from his belly. Avarice is a deadly sin."

- The sin should be condemned but the sinner should be called to repentance: "That at some time or other they may come to their senses … that they may repent, even at the last minute of their wicked crime … that they may deserve to live with God and be made well."

FOR YOUR FOLDER

1. Describe Patrick's call to return to Ireland.

2. Why did Patrick consider himself unworthy for the mission to Ireland?

3. Why did Patrick write his *Letter to Coroticus*?

4. In what ways does Patrick show himself to be a man of faith?

5. Summarise the main teachings of Patrick.

6. What do you think Christians today can learn from Patrick's teachings?

6. "Living the Christian faith today is more difficult than it was for Patrick." Do you agree or disagree. Give reasons for your answer showing that you have considered more than one point of view.

St Patrick's Festival

St Patrick's day is celebrated on the 17th of March. It was originally a religious holiday used for prayer and devotion, but became a popular festival for Irish settlers in America. It was in America that St Patrick's day became the celebration of all things Irish that it is today. The first recorded St Patrick's day parade was in Boston Massachusetts in 1737.

Since the 1990s, Ireland's St Patrick's day celebrations have grown into a five day festival celebrating Irish culture. Some of the biggest celebrations are to be found in Downpatrick, because of the town's connections with St Patrick.

ST PATRICK'S FESTIVAL

St Patrick's Festival was established by the Government of Ireland in November 1995.

The principle aim of St. Patrick's Festival, since its inauguration, is to develop a major annual international festival around the national holiday over which the 'owners' of the festival, the Irish people, would stand proud. It sets out to reflect the talents and achievements of Irish people on many national and world stages, and it acts as an exciting showcase for the manifold skills of the people of Ireland, of every age and social background.

Source: www.stpatricksfestival.ie

Riot police
called to disturbance

Twelve people have been arrested during disturbances in south Belfast.

Police were called at about 1500 GMT to Carmel Street in the Holylands area where a car had been vandalised. Hundreds of St Patrick's Day house parties in the area had spilled out on the streets, and a small minority threw cans and bottles at police… Local private homeowners said the disturbances proved there were too many shared houses, flats and multiple occupancies in the area.

Source: 'Riot police called to disturbance', bbc news, 17 march 2009, http://news.Bbc.Co.Uk/1/hi/northern_ireland/7949145. Stm, accessed 29 june 2009

IN A GROUP

Read the two articles on this page.

Using them as a starting point, research the St Patrick's Day celebrations throughout Ireland. You might find the following websites helpful:

www.stpatricksfestival.ie

www.st-patricksdayfestival.com

www.st-patricks-day.com

Discuss the following questions in relation to your findings.

1. Why do you think the disturbances in the Holylands occurred?

2. What could be done to prevent something like this happening again?

3. Do you think the St Patrick's Day celebrations in Ireland really celebrate the achievements of St Patrick? Give reasons for your answer.

Patrick the person

Patrick's writings show us that he was a very humble man. He believed that all he had achieved had come from God. Any abilities that he had developed were also gifts from God.

Ken Thompson's statue of 'Patrick the Pilgrim', an insightful portrayal of the young Patrick.

Patrick was very courageous. He remained in Ireland with his flock in spite of the many dangers and difficulties he faced. He was not afraid to speak out against the actions of Prince Coroticus even when he knew that it would make him unpopular with some very important people.

Patrick was also a good pastor and shepherd to his flock. He spoke up and identified himself with his Irish converts in the *Letter to Coroticus*. He made it clear that he was on their side. He was dedicated to remaining with the Irish for the rest of his life even if it meant he would never see his family or friends again. He was always concerned for those who were weakest among his converts, especially those who were in slavery.

Patrick was a prayerful man, saying as many as 100 prayers both day and night.

One of Patrick's most noteworthy qualities was that he was charitable. Despite how badly the Irish

treated him in the past he dedicated the rest of his life to them. Similarly, despite the actions of Coroticus and his men, he prayed that they would repent so that they could be united again with God and the Church.

IN A GROUP

1. What qualities do you think Patrick needed to carry out his mission to the Irish?
2. Why do you think that Patrick and not Palladius is the patron saint of Ireland?

HOW PROTESTANTISM EMERGED AS A RESULT OF THE REFORMATION

In the Middle Ages the Church in the Western World was not divided into different denominations as it is today. The Church in the west was Catholic, and the Pope was the head of the Church.

The Pope was a very powerful man, and it was believed that he could grant 'indulgences' which could take away some of the punishment expected by sinners. In the Middle Ages there was also a strong belief in purgatory, a place where Christians who had sinned went to immediately after death, before being admitted into heaven. The amount of time spent in purgatory depended on how much a Christian had sinned and on whether or not they had received an indulgence. It was possible to receive an indulgence on behalf of someone who had already died, thus lessening their suffering in the afterlife.

People could earn an indulgence by carrying out a religious act such as special prayers or making a charitable donation to the Church. The larger the donation, the more effective the indulgence. In time this meant that the Church was effectively selling God's forgiveness. The richer the person, the more forgiveness they could afford. When this happened, people began to question the practice of indulgences. Indulgences often took the form of signed documents promising forgiveness of sins or less time in purgatory. Not only could many people not read, the documents were all written in Latin, a language known by very few.

In 1510 a German monk called Martin Luther visited Rome and was appalled by the corruption he saw there. In 1517 the scandal caused by the sale of indulgences came to a head. A priest named Johann Tetzel came to Wittenberg in Germany asking for money in return for indulgences from the Pope. Luther's anger was roused by this because he was convinced that people only become right with God through faith in Christ and not by the good things that they try to do, or by paying money to the church.

Luther was furious and decided to take action to make the public aware of how he felt. Today if you want to attract people's attention about an important issue you might post an article on the internet. Back in the Middle Ages you could post an article on the door of the church. So Luther nailed a document (commonly referred to as Luther's '95 Theses') to the door of his church in Wittenberg. The document made strong allegations against the Catholic Church, and in particular it spoke out against the abuse of indulgences. Luther also questioned the power of the Pope and attacked some of the teachings of the church.

With the invention of the printing press many of Luther's ideas became widely known. He called for people to read the Bible for themselves, arguing that scripture alone, and not the teaching of the church, was the word of God.

With the debate out in the open, many people agreed with Luther in calling for change in the church. They began to look directly to the Bible for answers, arguing that salvation is by faith alone. These Christians 'protested' at the way the Church was run and some things that were taught. They became known as 'Protestants' because of their protests.

Luther spent the rest of his life spreading his ideas through his writings. In 1534 he published a complete translation of the Bible into German, which supported his belief that people should be able to read it in their own language.

FOR YOUR FOLDER

1. Give a definition of an 'Indulgence'.

2. Why was Martin Luther angry about the practice of Indulgences?

3. Explain why Martin Luther was supported by other Christians.

4. Describe the origin of the term 'Protestant'.

5. Do you think it is important for people today to understand differences between the beliefs of Protestants and Catholics?

IN A GROUP

1. What issues might cause controversy and division in the Church today?

2. Do you think the Church is good at dealing with controversial issues?

FURTHER THINKING

The reformation was not confined to Germany. Other Catholics started protest movements against the church. Find more information about the following people and write a paragraph summarising their work:

England: Thomas Cranmer (1489–1556)
France: John Calvin (1509–1564)

Chapter 2

CHURCH GOVERNMENT

MODELS OF CHURCH GOVERNMENT

Church government refers to how a church is led and organised. Some churches are very highly organised while others are more flexible and less structured.

There are three main types of church government:

1. The episcopal model

This form of church government developed in the first three centuries, following the death and Resurrection of Jesus. You will remember from chapter one of this book that the very early Church was charismatic and people were spontaneous when it came to worship and organisation. They dealt with issues as the need arose. However, as time passed Christians were persecuted by the Roman Emperors. It became increasingly important to have strong leadership in the Church and to be united to provide a strong defence against attack.

It is around this time that the Church became more structured. Bishops took on vital roles in leading and maintaining unity in the Church. The term 'bishop' comes from the Greek word *episcopoi* which means 'overseer'. Today, churches organised using the **episcopal model** are governed by bishops. Each bishop is in charge of a geographical area called a diocese, which consists of a number of local or parish churches. There is a clear line of command or hierarchy in the episcopal model.

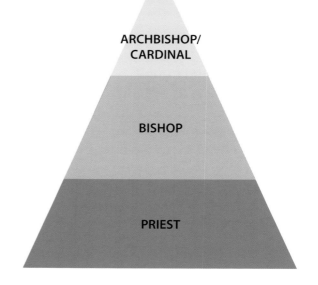

The Roman Catholic Church and the Church of Ireland both follow an episcopal model.

2. The representative model

This form of church government first appeared at the time of the Reformation. There are no bishops in this model, although it is highly organised. Decisions are made by councils that are made up of church leaders (clergy and laity) who represent the opinions of their congregation. It is a two-way process, where all church members have a chance to let their voices be heard.

During the Reformation there was a complaint that many of the bishops and priests in the Catholic Church were abusing their power. When people broke away from the Catholic Church it was decided to use a representative model of government to prevent this sort of abuse happening again. An example of the representative model is the Presbyterian Church.

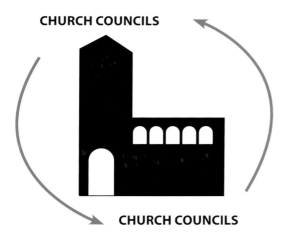

CHURCH COUNCILS

CHURCH COUNCILS

3. The congregational model

This model also emerged at the time of the Reformation. The idea behind it is that all Christians are equal and should answer to God alone. In this model power is placed in the hands of the church members. Everyone who belongs to the church is regarded as equal. No one is more important than anyone else. It is argued that this reflects the early church as described in Acts.

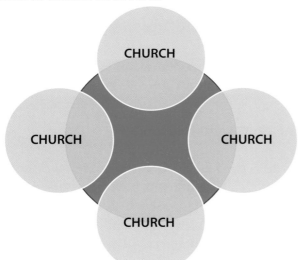

CHURCH

CHURCH

CHURCH

CHURCH

While each individual church in this model is free to make its own decisions, there is contact and understanding with other churches within the model. These churches have shared beliefs and often follow similar patterns for worship. An example of the congregational model is the Baptist Church.

IN A GROUP

1. Do you think it is important for a church to have one strong leader? Give reasons for your answer.

2. Which of the models described do you think works best in the twenty-first century?

3. Some Christians might decide to opt out of these models of government altogether and worship with friends and family at home. What reasons could there be for this?

LEADERSHIP

Depending on the type of church government, Christian congregations are led in a variety of ways. Some groups have no definite leader, with each individual member seeking God's will and all having an equal input into the life of the church. Other groups have a hierarchy of leadership as seen in the episcopal model.

Often, church leaders are referred to by special titles. In the New Testament the titles bishop, presbyter, elder, overseer and deacon were all used. Each office had a particular job to do.

FURTHER THINKING

You already know that the word 'bishop' means 'overseer'. Use the internet or a library to find out what is meant by these words:

| Presbyter | Pastor | Vicar |
| Rector | Minister | Priest |

IN A GROUP

1. Read Philippians 1:1; 1 Timothy 3:1–8; Titus 1:5–8 and 1 Peter 5:1–2.

2. Make a list of the qualities someone had to possess to be able to hold an office in the early Church.

3. Do you think these qualities should be a requirement for leaders in the Church today?

ORDINATION

To be ordained means to be appointed or set apart. Ordination is the act by which the church sets apart leaders to serve in particular offices (usually that of priest or minister). This usually happens at a special church service. The word 'ordination' is derived from 'order'. In ordination the church orders its ministry.

The debate about the ordination of women

Christian denominations disagree when it comes to female leaders, priests and pastors. Some believe that only men should be in particular leadership roles in the Church. Others argue that many women are also good leaders, and should be allowed to serve the Church in this way. Both sides of the debate present strong cases.

Currently, each denomination has different beliefs about the ordination of women:

- The Presbyterian Church in Ireland has ordained women as elders since 1926. The ordination of women to the 'ministry of the word and sacrament' (preaching, baptism and communion) was agreed by the General Assembly in 1973. Dr Ruth Patterson made history in the 1970s when she became the first woman to be ordained to the Presbyterian ministry in Ireland. A woman has never been elected as moderator of the General Assembly.

- The Methodist Church has had women ministers for over 30 years (since 1977).

- In recent years the Church of Ireland has decided to allow women priests or ministers. The debate over whether women should be bishops continues.

- The Catholic Church remains strongly opposed to the idea of women as priests. Women

have always been able to become nuns or religious sisters in the Catholic Church. Some have a lot of responsibility but they are not allowed to become priests:

> "The Church, in fidelity to the example of the Lord, does not consider itself authorised to admit women to priestly ordination" (Congregation of the doctrine of the Faith, 1976).

The issue of accepting women into the priesthood in the Catholic Church remains a controversial issue. In 1994, Pope John Paul II announced in an apostolic letter on ordination that the ban would continue, was definitive and not open to debate among Catholics.

The article below shows just how serious an issue this is for many people:

PRIEST GETS POSTCARD DEATH THREAT

In 2008 a woman priest in the Church of England found a death threat written on a postcard which was hidden in her Bible in church. The postcard warned the priest that she would die unless she left the church.

The previous year the 54 year old had letters sent to her home expressing anger that she was a clergywoman. A lit candle was thrown into her car and another candle was left burning in the porch of her house, causing logs stored there to ignite.

One of her parishioners commented: "It is appalling that somebody who would claim to be a Christian could take such a warped and perverted view of their faith and think they have a moral right to do this."

The priest started work as a curate in 2006. The intimidation against her began when she began leading services after the retirement of the previous male parish priest.

Following the postcard death threat the priest decided to take a break from her duties.

IN A GROUP

1. Do you think the priest was right to take a break from her duties?
2. What could be done to help a female priest in similar circumstances?
3. Do you think women should avoid becoming priests for their own safety?

CLASS DEBATE

Look at the following arguments for and against the ordination of women.

Prepare for a class debate:

"This house believes that women should accept men as their leaders in the church."

ARGUMENTS AGAINST	ARGUMENTS FOR
It is a tradition that goes back to the very first Christians. Jesus had many women followers, but Jesus chose all men to be his disciples. It is important that the Church follows this tradition.	God created men and women in his likeness, not just men.
Some churches use the Apostle Paul's teachings to support their view of the role of women in the church today. Paul viewed the role of women as being different to that of men: *"But I want you to understand that Christ is supreme over every man, the husband is supreme over his wife, and God is supreme over Christ"* (1 Corinthians 11:3). *"… the women should keep quiet in the meetings. They are not allowed to speak; as the Jewish Law says, they must not be in charge. If they want to find out something, they should ask their husbands at home. It is a disgraceful thing for a woman to speak in a church meeting"* (1 Corinthians 14:34–35).	Jesus had a radical attitude to women. In a society where women were treated as second-class citizens, Jesus talked to them openly, treating them with respect and dignity. Some of Jesus' closest companions were women.
A priest's role is to represent Christ when he stands at the altar. Christ was a man.	Jesus chose twelve male disciples in a culture where women usually stayed at home and were not permitted to speak in public. The situation in the western world today is completely different.
Read **1 Timothy 2:8–15.** This teaches that women are second to men. Men should lead and women should follow.	There are a number of female leaders in the Bible and in the very early Church. The prophet Deborah lead Israel (Judges 4 & 5), Romans 16:1 refers to a female deacon, Phoebe and Romans 16:7 mentions that Junia (a woman's name) is outstanding among the apostles.
Women have a number of important roles in the Church including caring ministries, hospitality, and passing on the faith at home. This is how they share in the ministry of Christ, rather than by ordination.	Read **Galatians 3:28.** This teaches that people should not be treated differently because of their gender.

THE PRIESTHOOD OF ALL BELIEVERS

This is the belief that every Christian shares in Christ's role as priest.

In the Protestant Church the view is that all Christians are priests and no special powers are given to a Christian through ordination. Ordination is simply an appointment to a full-time ministry and does not make its recipient any more of a priest than any other Christian.

For example, in the Methodist and Presbyterian Churches ordination takes place because it is believed that the church should carefully select its ministers. In the Baptist Church there is no ordained ministry. Leaders are usually chosen from the congregation itself or from another congregation.

Similarly, the Catholic Church teaches that all Christians are called to share in Christ's priestly role. However, those who are called to the priesthood are ordained in a special way and are consecrated by the laying on of hands. Ordination gives special authority to the priest. For example, only a priest (and those of higher rank) has the power to consecrate the bread and wine in the sacrament of the Eucharist. A priest alone can forgive sins in the name of God.

CHURCH ORGANISATION

CHURCH GOVERNMENT IN THE CATHOLIC CHURCH

Church government in the Catholic Church is episcopal. The Catholic Church has archbishops, bishops, and priests. The head of the Catholic Church is the Pope (the Bishop of Rome).

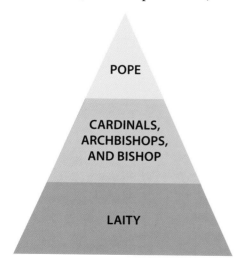

During the second Vatican Council (1962–1965), the Catholic Church emphasised the idea of Church as the people of God rather than just the hierarchy or the building. Some people favour this less hierarchical understanding of the Catholic Church:

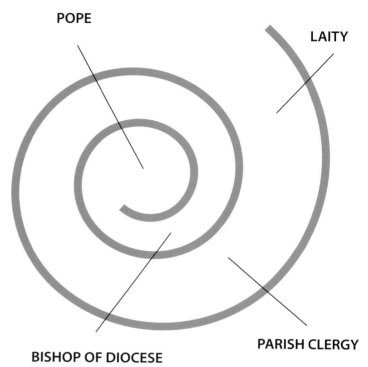

POPE

LAITY

BISHOP OF DIOCESE

PARISH CLERGY

DECISION-MAKING BODIES

The Pope

The Catholic Church believes that the Pope is the successor of the disciple Peter and has been given a special and unique role of leadership and authority. He can speak for the whole Church. The Catholic Church believes that the Pope is infallible. This means that when the Pope is speaking in a formal way about a matter of faith, he is without even the possibility of error. Through the action of the Holy Spirit he solemnly declares something to be a matter of faith, which all Catholics must accept.

NOTE

If the Pope is making an infallible statement he usually begins with a phrase like "we decree ..."

Did you know?

Two recent infallible statements were in 1854 when Pope Pius IX decreed the Immaculate Conception of Mary (that Mary was conceived without the ability to sin) and in 1950 Pius XII declared the Assumption of Mary into Heaven (that Mary was taken up into heaven rather than dying normally). These became articles of faith to be accepted by all Catholics.

IN A GROUP

Discuss the advantages and disadvantages of a having an infallible leader.

The Ecumenical Council

This is made up of the 'College of Bishops'. As a group they are regarded as the direct descendants of the Apostles and therefore have authority to govern the Church. The Ecumenical Council makes clear the teaching and beliefs of the Catholic Church. The meeting of the Ecumenical Council is a very solemn gathering of the bishops of the world. They meet to discuss matters of faith and church discipline with the Pope when he invites them to do so. There have been only 21 of these Ecumenical Councils in the history of the Church. The second Vatican Council, which met between 11 October 1962 and 8 December 1965, was the most recent meeting of the Ecumenical Council. When it meets with the Pope to agree teaching, the Ecumenical Council is the highest authority in the Catholic Church.

The Magisterium

This is the name given to the teaching authority of the Catholic Church. It is made up of the bishops of the Church led by the Pope. Their role is to teach and interpret the truths of the faith.

College of Cardinals

The college's roles are to assist the Pope in governing the Church, manage the Vatican in the absence of the Pope and to elect a new Pope on the death of a Pope.

The Curia

This is a body that assists the Pope in all practical administrative duties. It is located in the Vatican.

Parish Councils

These operate at local level and are made up of lay people who assist the priest in the practical running of the parish. They may organise fundraising activities, church collections, or even plan and prepare some aspects of worship, for example in a liturgical group.

FOR YOUR FOLDER

1. Explain what Papal infallibility means.

2. What is the role of the Curia?

3. What is an Ecumenical Council?

4. Why do Catholics believe that the Pope has a special and unique role of leadership?

5. Describe how the Catholic Church is organised at either local or national level.

PERSONNEL IN CATHOLIC CHURCH

Pope

The Pope is head of the worldwide Roman Catholic Church. He lives in the Vatican in Rome because it is believed that that is where Peter, the first Pope, is buried.

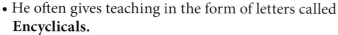

- He has final authority in all matters.
- He appoints bishops to their dioceses or transfers them to another diocese.
- He often gives teaching in the form of letters called **Encyclicals.**

Cardinals

Cardinals hold the highest office of dignity in the Catholic Church after the Pope. They are appointed by the Pope from among the ranks of bishops.

- They form the Sacred College of Cardinals who gather in the Sistine Chapel in Rome to elect a new Pope.
- Some work in the Vatican while others are bishops of dioceses.

Bishops

Bishops are in charge of dioceses.

- They confer the Sacrament of Ordination.
- They appoint priests to parishes within the dioceses and other duties, and lead and support them.
- They bless the oils for the Anointing of the sick and the Oil of Chrism at a special Mass on Holy Thursday.
- They usually administer the Sacrament of Confirmation (although may at times delegate it to a priest).
- They preach the Gospel to their people and ensure that the Sacraments are offered to them.
- Only bishops can consecrate a church or bless altars.

Archbishops

The archbishop is the name given to a bishop who rules over a particularly large diocese or one which incorporates a capital city. He does not have greater authority than a bishop. The archbishop who acts as the official delegate or representative of the Vatican for a country is called the **Papal Nuncio.**

Priest

Priests are directly under the authority of the bishop. They minister in parishes.

- They preach the Gospel.
- They consecrate the bread and wine at Mass.
- They celebrate the sacraments in parishes, schools, hospitals and prisons.
- They care for the needs of the people of the parish.
- They assist and are obedient to the bishop.
- Some priests are given the title **monsignor** in recognition of their particular contribution to the Church.

Deacons

Deacons are ordained members of the clergy under bishops and priests. A man is ordained deacon the year before he is ordained priest.

- They help priests in parishes.
- They can read the Gospel and preach the sermon.
- They distribute Communion.

Men and women in religious orders

These can be religious sisters, brothers, priests or nuns.

- They live in community under the vows of poverty, chastity and obedience.
- They usually work in pastoral ministry, perhaps in schools, hospitals or among the poor.
- **Nuns** are different from religious sisters because they are **Contemplative** or enclosed and their ministry is to pray for the Church.

Laity

The laity in the Catholic Church have become more and more active in a practical way in parishes by:

- Sitting on the parish council.

- Helping to organise liturgy.
- Reading at Mass.
- Being Eucharistic ministers (giving the Eucharist to the congregation during Mass or bringing it to the elderly or infirm when they cannot attend church).
- Working in pastoral ministry in catechesis (preparing people for sacraments).

FOR YOUR FOLDER

1. Explain the role of the Pope in the Catholic Church.
2. What does the bishop in charge of a diocese do?
3. In what way does the role of Cardinal differ from that of bishop?
4. What is a deacon and what role does he carry out?
5. What is the difference between a religious sister and a nun?
6. Do you think it is important that lay people have a role in the church? Give reasons for your answer.

Clerical celibacy

Priests in the Catholic Church are celibate. That means they do not marry. The issue of clerical celibacy is frequently debated especially when there is a shortage of priests. Several arguments can be put forward both for and against clerical celibacy.

Did you know?

Clerical celibacy in the Catholic Church was introduced in the eleventh century. Before that priests could marry.

ARGUMENTS FOR CLERICAL CELIBACY

If he is unmarried he can be more available for his people.

Giving up marriage and family is a sacrifice for the sake of God and the Church.

He is more flexible and can be moved around from one parish to another as needed.

He is less of a financial burden on the church without a wife or children.

It is a sign of his total dedication to his ministry.

It means he is free to love all God's people equally, not one in particular.

ARGUMENTS AGAINST CLERICAL CELIBACY

Marriage is a basic human right.

A married priest would be more understanding of family and better able to help his parishioners.

Celibacy has good points but it should be optional.

Priests were allowed to get married in the early church.

If marriage were allowed there might be more young men opting for the priesthood.

Clerical celibacy can give the impression that sex and sexuality is something negative.

IN A GROUP

Can you think of any other arguments for or against clerical celibacy?

A DAY IN THE LIFE OF A PRIEST

… It was 3.30 am when the sound of the phone woke Father Peter. It was the police to say that there had been had been a serious car accident on the main Larne to Antrim road. A man had been hurt but was conscious. He had asked for a priest to hear his Confession and give him the Sacrament of the Sick. "It is a cold night", thought Father Peter, "the roads are icy. It isn't surprising that there had been an accident". Father Peter pulled on an extra jumper as he braved the cold January night. In ten minutes he arrived and found the man still conscious in the care of the paramedics. He anointed him with oil and heard his confession. The man was anxious that Father Peter, rather than the police, would tell his wife about the accident. Father Peter assured him he would tell her and made the 15 mile journey to the man's home.

It was 5.00 am when Father Peter arrived home. He phoned the hospital to check on the man and was told he was comfortable. He would go to the hospital later and visit the man and a few other parishioners who were sick. He made himself a cup of tea and a slice of toast. He would just have time to say his Morning Prayer before it would be time to go to lead the 8.00 am Mass. It was the Feast of the Epiphany so there were extra Masses today; another at 11.30 am and 8.00 pm tonight.

After the morning Mass he met with Joe the sacristan who took care of the Church. There was a problem with the heating system and Joe wanted to know what they do about it. Father Peter promised to look into it. It was 10.00 am and Father Peter thought he would just have time to read over the agenda for tonight's parish Council meeting before the next Mass. He would have to add the church heating to the list! After the 11.30 am Mass he headed to the local Grammar school. He was to say lunchtime Mass there for the pupils and staff. He could do his hospital visitation on the way back.

At 5.00 pm Father Peter made his way home. Mrs Kelly the housekeeper had his dinner ready. It had been a long time since that cup of tea and slice of toast. He noticed there was a message from the bishop, a call he would have to return immediately. At the end of the call some parishioners came to the door. They wanted to spend an hour or so going through the plans they had for their wedding Mass in four weeks time. Before he knew it he was on his way to the 8.00 pm Mass, followed by that Parish Council meeting. He knew it would be a long one, with so much to get through.

At 11.00 pm Father Peter returned home again. It had been a long day …

IN A GROUP

1. Read the story above, then discuss what the story tells you about the life and role of a priest.

2. Look again at the arguments for and against clerical celibacy. Do you think this story has any relevance to the debate about clerical celibacy? Give reasons for your answers.

CHURCH GOVERNMENT IN THE CHURCH OF IRELAND

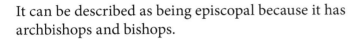

Church government in the Church of Ireland can be referred to as both episcopal and representative. Remember that the word 'episcopal' refers to a bishop.

It can be described as being episcopal because it has archbishops and bishops.

It can be described as being representative because no one person has absolute power. Decisions are the responsibility of clergy and laity. There is a General Synod made up of clergy and lay representatives from local churches, elected every three years by the twelve Diocesan Synods, which meet once a year, for three days, to make decisions.

DECISION-MAKING BODIES

General Synod

Chair person: archbishop

Those who are elected to the General Synod represent the clergy and laity of the Church of Ireland. Clergy comprise one-third and laity two-thirds of the membership. It is made up of The House of Bishops, The House of Clergy (rectors or ministers) and House of Laity (ordinary church members). Everyone's vote carries equal weight. However, certain issues require a majority in the House of Clergy and the House of Laity voting separately. The General Synod is the authoritative decision-making body of the Church of Ireland, and is responsible for all the laws of the Church.

There are other committees in the Church of Ireland which carry on the work of the General Synod throughout the year.

Diocesan Synod

Chair person: bishop

Representatives from each parish church within a diocese meet in the Diocesan Synod. The Synod is chaired by the bishop and attended by clergy (rectors, curates, etc) and lay people (ordinary church members). Decisions made at the General Synod are passed on to the Diocesan Synod. Other matters of concern to the diocese are also considered. Matters that the diocese feels should be brought before the General Synod are also discussed.

Select Vestry

Chair person: rector

Each parish church has a Select Vestry of 16 members – 2 appointed by the Rector, 14 elected by the Annual General Vestry of the parish. These ordinary members of the church help the clergy (rectors) to run the church. They are responsible for different issues, such as finance and property, and are increasingly consulted by the Rector on a broad range of issues. The rector of the parish chairs meetings.

The Church of Ireland is a member Church of the Anglican Communion of Churches, which has a worldwide membership of 80 million. Many Parish churches and groups are twinned with Anglican Churches around the world. There is also extensive partnership between the Church of Ireland and the Lutheran Episcopal Churches of Scandinavia and the Baltic republics.

FOR YOUR FOLDER

1. Describe how the Church of Ireland is organised at either local or national level

2. Explain how the Church of Ireland is both episcopal and representative.

3. What is the difference between the General Synod and the Diocesan Synod?

4. Do you think it is important for the Church of Ireland to be connected to other Anglican churches?

PERSONNEL IN THE CHURCH OF IRELAND

There are three main positions of leadership, or Orders, in the Church of Ireland: bishop, priest (minister or rector) and deacon.

Archbishop Desmond Tutu was leader of the Anglican Church of Southern Africa

Bishop

The bishop is the leader of the local diocese. His main responsibilities include:

- To 'guard the faith'
- To ensure the sacraments are properly administered
- To ordain
- To confirm

Priest (minister or rector)

The parish priest cares for his own congregation and is sometimes assisted by a curate (assistant). Some of the duties carried out by the parish priest include:

- Preaching and teaching
- Preparation for baptism and marriage
- Funerals
- School visits
- Home and hospital visits
- Chairing of committee meetings

Deacon

A deacon in the Church of Ireland is a trainee minister who helps the priest for one year before ordination to the Priesthood. He or she may assist at Holy Communion and at baptisms. Other duties include youth work and visiting the sick and elderly.

FOR YOUR FOLDER

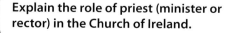

Explain the role of priest (minister or rector) in the Church of Ireland.

FURTHER THINKING

Interview a priest (minister or rector) in the Church of Ireland to find out what a typical week's work would involve.

CHURCH GOVERNMENT IN THE BAPTIST CHURCH

The Baptist Church is an example of the congregational model. There is no formal structure of government in the Baptist Church, with each church regarding itself as independent. However, Baptist churches make an effort to work with each other and therefore they can also be described as **inter-dependent.**

Many Baptist churches in Ireland work together as part of the Association of Baptist Churches. It supports the work of individual churches through involvement in:

- Missionary work
- Youth work
- Education
- Care for the poor

Twice a year each individual Baptist church sends a representative to a Church Council, which oversees the work of the Association. Some Baptist churches choose not to join the Association. They are known as **independent** Baptist churches.

In each individual Baptist Church there is a group of elders who lead the church and take part in pastoral duties, for example, visiting the sick. If an important decision has to be made it is brought before the church members at a members' meeting. For very important decisions there must be two-thirds of the church membership present for a vote to be valid.

PERSONNEL IN THE BAPTIST CHURCH

The Baptist Church is led by a group of elders. One of these elders, the teaching elder, is known as the Pastor. The Pastor is usually employed to work for the church full-time.

Some Baptist Churches have moved towards the idea of team ministry, where the church employs a Pastor, an assistant Pastor and maybe a church worker. Each person would take on different responsibilities to help share the workload.

Elder

The elders are regarded as the spiritual leaders and are elected by the congregation. They are expected to have good character and be spiritually mature.

Normally the only elder with a full-time position in the church is the teaching elder (Pastor). The remaining elders support the church in various ways, for example, providing pastoral care.

Pastor

There is normally one pastor for each Baptist Church, although some of the larger churches have more than one. Some of the duties carried out by the Pastor include:

- Preaching and teaching
- Mid-week Bible study
- Home and hospital visits
- Leadership in committees

Deacon

Deacons look after the practical work of the church, such as finance and maintenance of the church building.

FOR YOUR FOLDER

1. Describe how the Baptist Church is organised at either local or national level.

2. Describe the work of the Association of Baptist Churches.

3. Explain how Baptist Churches are both independent and inter-dependent.

4. What is an Independent Baptist Church?

5. Explain the role of Pastor in the Baptist Church.

6. Who do you think benefits from a team ministry?

FURTHER THINKING

Interview a Pastor in the Baptist Church to find out what a typical week's work would involve.

CHURCH GOVERNMENT IN THE METHODIST CHURCH

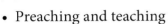

The Methodist Church in Ireland follows the representative model of church government. Methodists describe their form of government as being 'connexional' (connected). The highest decision-making body in the Methodist Church is the Conference. There is a strong link between what happens here and the wishes of ordinary church members.

DECISION-MAKING BODIES

Methodist Conference

This is the main decision-making body. There are equal numbers of ministers and lay people (ordinary church members). The president of the Methodist Church is elected at the conference and serves for one year. Everyone has the same voting rights.

District Synod

In Ireland the Methodist Church is divided into eight districts at present. Each district is led by a superintendent minister (elected every three years) who chairs a meeting of ministers and leaders in the district. Issues are discussed that may be passed on to the Conference. The District Synod is also responsible for the management of church property and the development of worship in the district.

Circuit Executive

Each district is made up of circuits (a number of churches) which are headed by a superintendent minister. Decisions made by local societies (churches) must be agreed at the Circuit Executive.

Church Council

Each individual church is called a society. There is a Church Council, which makes decisions concerning societies. This is attended by the local minister and church leaders.

The Methodist Church in Ireland has links with other Methodist churches around the world. Such links are often maintained through the sending and receiving of missionary partners.

FOR YOUR FOLDER

1. Describe how the Methodist church is organised at either local or national level.
2. Explain how the Methodist Church in Ireland is 'connexional'.
3. What advantages are there to this model of government?

PERSONNEL IN THE METHODIST CHURCH

The personnel in the Methodist Church include superintendent ministers, ministers and local preachers.

Superintendents

In the Methodist Church a 'church' is referred to as a 'society'. A 'group of churches' is referred to as a 'circuit'. A superintendent is responsible for a circuit. Some of the churches within a circuit may not have a minister. They rely upon voluntary ministers. These can be retired ministers who work part-time for the church.

Minister

A minister in the Methodist Church can be male or female. In 1977, the Reverend Ellen Whalley was the first woman ordained into the Methodist Church in Ireland. Some of the duties carried out by the minister include:

- Preaching and teaching
- Prayer
- Pastoral visits to the sick and elderly
- Chairing committee meetings
- Working in the local community
- School visits

Local preacher

A local preacher is an ordinary church member who receives training and qualifies to preach in the Methodist Church. They take Sunday services and usually have another career.

Some of the other roles in the Methodist Church include society steward (supports the minister), class leaders (home visits), family workers, community workers and youth workers.

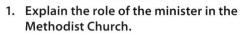
FOR YOUR FOLDER

1. Explain the role of the minister in the Methodist Church.
2. What would be the benefits of having local preachers?

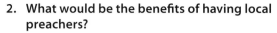
FURTHER THINKING

Interview a minister in the Methodist Church to find out what a typical week's work would involve.

CHURCH GOVERNMENT IN THE PRESBYTERIAN CHURCH

The Presbyterian Church in Ireland follows the representative model of church government. There are four main decision-making bodies.

DECISION-MAKING BODIES

General Assembly

Major decisions concerning issues like mission and education are made at the General Assembly which meets once a year. Each congregation sends one minister and one elder. Both have equal voting rights. The Assembly is chaired by the Moderator who is elected annually.

Synod

There are five regional synods in Ireland. Each congregation sends one minister and one elder to the annual meeting in their region.

Presbytery

There are 21 presbyteries in Ireland, with about 24 churches in each presbytery. Each congregation sends one minister and one elder to the presbytery meetings. There are around 8 meetings a year. Local business is dealt with, as well as any issues that come directly from the General Assembly.

Kirk Session

The Kirk Session is the name given to the committee that meets to make decisions for each individual

Presbyterian congregation. Members include the elected elders and the minister.

The Presbyterian Church in Ireland maintains links with other Presbyterian Churches, such as the Church of Scotland. It also has international links with churches in Africa, Eastern Europe and the USA.

FOR YOUR FOLDER

1. Describe how the Presbyterian Church is organised at either local or national level.
2. What do you think are the advantages and disadvantages of the way the Presbyterian Church is governed?
3. Explain how the Presbyterian Church follows a representative model.

PERSONNEL IN THE PRESBYTERIAN CHURCH

Personnel in the Presbyterian Church include ministers, elders and deaconesses.

Minister

The minister in the Presbyterian Church does not have any special power or authority. He or she has the same relationship with God as other Christians in their church. The minister is expected however, to have the gift of teaching and preaching:

"They that are called to labour in the ministry of the word are to preach sound doctrine, diligently … plainly … faithfully … wisely … zealously [and] sincerely". (Larger Catechism A.159)

The minister is therefore referred to as the teaching elder. There is normally at least one minister assigned to each Presbyterian Church. In many churches there is also an assistant minister (in training for his or her own church); and sometimes an associate minister (someone ordained but who does not have a congregation of their own). Some of the duties carried out by the minister include:

- Preaching and teaching
- Pastoral duties, such as visiting the sick, home visits, school visits and hospital visits
- Funerals
- Administration
- Chairing meetings of the Kirk Session (elders)

Elder

There are a number of elders, male and female, in each Presbyterian Church. An elder has the same authority in the church as the minister. While the minister works full time for the church the elders have their own jobs outside the church. The minister is also responsible for preaching, carrying out the sacraments of baptisms and communion, and officiating at wedding ceremonies and funerals. Each elder is appointed to look after a number of families in the church. Some of their duties include:

- Home visits
- Giving communion tokens
- Supporting the minister, for example; by helping to serve communion or reading the Bible lesson at worship services

Deaconess

A deaconess carries out the same sort of work that a minister does, except preaching and administering the sacraments of baptism and communion. There is no male equivalent.

FOR YOUR FOLDER

1. Explain the role of minister in the Presbyterian Church.
2. What do you see as the benefits of having elders?

FURTHER THINKING

Interview a minister in the Presbyterian Church to find out what a typical week's work would involve.

FOR YOUR FOLDER

Describe the system of Church government in one Christian tradition you have studied.

Chapter 3

CHRISTIAN WORSHIP

STYLES OF WORSHIP

Christian worship means showing adoration to God. Worship is not just about singing hymns of praise to God but can also involve prayer, movement and fellowship together. Some Christians would even regard their whole way of life as a form of worship.

No two Christian denominations are the same when it comes to how congregations worship God. Throughout Christian history there have been disagreements over the best way to express worship. Even within one denomination people may differ in how they prefer to worship.

LITURGICAL, STRUCTURED WORSHIP

This style of worship follows a clear pattern at every worship service. It uses pre-written prayers and creeds, contained in special books or printed on leaflets. The term used for written prayers, creeds and instructions for worship is **liturgy**. Catholic and Church of Ireland churches are most likely to use this style of worship. In the Catholic Church they use the *Missal,* while the Church of Ireland use the *Book of Common Prayer,* or the more modern *Alternative Prayer Book.*

Other Christian denominations may not use a special book but their worship services are still very structured

and follow a general routine. Examples include the Baptist Church and the Presbyterian Church. This means that the same order is used from one week to the next. Prayers tend not to be set and differ from one week to the next. This style of worship is orderly but there is also opportunity for variety.

Why do some people prefer liturgical worship?

- The idea of liturgy is based on the Bible. In the Old Testament the Israelites were commanded to recite special words when making offerings (Deuteronomy 26:3–15) and in the New Testament Jesus uses the Lord's Prayer or 'Our Father' as an example of how to pray. This prayer is frequently used during liturgy in churches today.
- Some people feel that speaking to God should be done in a very respectful manner. The best way to do this is to use pre-written words.
- It is part of the tradition of the Church, to be passed down from one generation to the next.
- The congregation gets to play an active role in the worship service through reciting words and responding to prayers. They do not sit passively throughout the service; they have the opportunity to stand, sit, kneel, and go up to the front to receive communion.

NON-LITURGICAL, SPONTANEOUS WORSHIP

There are two types of non-liturgical or spontaneous worship:

1. **Leaderless worship**
   Some Christian denominations, such as the Brethren or Quakers, choose not to have a

minister or priest to lead their worship services. Instead anyone can contribute if they feel led to do so (although this does not apply to women in the Brethren Church). So someone might say a prayer, give a Bible reading or even preach a sermon without it having been planned in advance. This is spontaneous worship.

2. Pentecostal or 'Charismatic'

This style of worship is lively and impulsive. Features include clapping, dancing and sometimes flag-waving, as well as singing.

The word 'charismatic' comes from a Greek word, *charis*, which means 'gift', referring to the gifts of the Holy Spirit (1 Corinthians 12:1–14). Three examples of gifts still in use today are:

- The gift of tongues – worshipping using a heavenly language
- The gift of prophecy – speaking God's words
- The gift of healing – helping to heal people with physical, emotional or mental illness

Why do some people prefer spontaneous worship?

- It is similar to the worship of the very early Church of the New Testament.
- Some believe that worship should be joyful, exciting and uplifting.
- Some people find following a liturgy boring or restrictive.
- It follows the example of worship given in the Psalms: *"Praise the Lord! Sing a new song to the Lord … Praise him with dancing; play drums and harps in praise of him"* (Psalm 149:1–3).

FOR YOUR FOLDER

1. Describe two different styles of worship.
2. Explain why some people might prefer each of these styles.
3. Which style of worship would you prefer and why?

Speaking in Tongues

The spiritual gift of 'Speaking in Tongues' is first found in Acts chapter 2. It is also known as 'glossolalia', which comes from the Greek term *glossa*, meaning 'tongue'. It is a 'language miracle', where the Holy Spirit enables someone to speak in an unknown language.

Speaking in tongues is still common in some churches today. The gift is used in two ways:

1. In private prayer to God. Speaking or singing in a heavenly language can help people to communicate their thoughts and feelings to God.

2. In public worship services, where the message given in tongues must be accompanied by an interpretation for the whole congregation to understand. Just as some Christians have the gift of speaking in tongues, others have the gift of interpretation.

Amy, a Christian belonging to the Elim Pentecostal church, describes her experience of speaking in tongues:

"It is like a new language. At first you start off with just a few words and gradually your vocabulary grows. I speak in tongues more in private prayer than I do in church. It is a special way of being close to God. It is an experience of great joy. When I speak in tongues I feel really happy and sometimes I feel so happy that I cry…"

Do you know of any churches today where 'speaking in tongues' is still considered to be an important part of the worship service?

FOR YOUR FOLDER

1. Read Acts 2:1–11. Describe how the gift of speaking in tongues was used on the Day of Pentecost.

2. Do you think the gift of speaking in tongues is useful or beneficial for the Christian Church?

3. "Some people argue that the experience of speaking in tongues has no place in the church today." Do you agree or disagree? Give reasons for your answer.

FURTHER THINKING

Research the internet to find out how Christians today experience the gift of speaking in tongues.

THE TRADITION OF SINGING AND MUSIC

Singing songs of praise and worship to God has always been an important part of Christian worship. In some denominations everyone takes part in singing (for example, Presbyterian, Methodist and Church of Ireland); in others it may be the choir only that sings (for example, the Catholic Church).

There are various types of songs used in worship:

- **Traditional hymns**
  A hymn is a song of praise to God. Many churches have a strong tradition of singing hymns. For example, Charles Wesley, one of the founders of Methodism, wrote over 7,000 hymns, which are still used in different churches today.

- **Psalms**
  Psalms are songs of praise and worship found in the Old Testament. These have been put into verse form in a book called the *Psalter*. This makes them easy to set to music.

Singing Psalms is popular in many Presbyterian churches.

- **Choruses**
  These are songs which use everyday language and mainly appeal to younger Christians. They often accompany hymn singing and are collected in books, for example, *Mission Praise*.

- **Contemporary Worship**
  In many churches, worship is led by a band. The music could include many different styles. New praise and worship songs are being written all the time.

There are various types of musical instrument used in worship services, depending upon the denomination:

- **Organ**
  This is a keyboard instrument and is one of the oldest musical instruments in western society. It uses wind moving through pipes of various materials to produce sounds which can vary widely in tone and volume. In many denominations singing is led by the organist, as well as the choir. Organs are a common feature in larger church buildings and cathedrals.

- **Choir**

Many churches have a choir to lead the congregation in worship. As well as taking a lead in worship services, the choir can put on special events and normally work hard on their music for special occasions like Christmas and Easter. In a few Catholic churches there may be some very traditional choirs which sing in Latin.

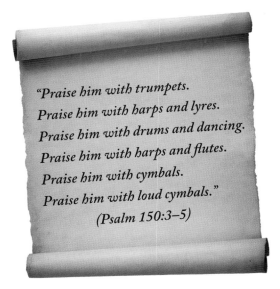

"Praise him with trumpets.
Praise him with harps and lyres.
Praise him with drums and dancing.
Praise him with harps and flutes.
Praise him with cymbals.
Praise him with loud cymbals."
(Psalm 150:3–5)

- **Band**

In some churches, worship is almost always led by a band. In other denominations instruments appear only on particular occasions such as **Folk Masses** in the Catholic Church. Church bands tend to be guitar-based, but can feature drums, violins, flutes, trumpets or any instrument. Some churches even count DJs and VJs as part of their worship team.

The Presbyterian Church recognises the importance of singing:

"The singing of praise is another important part of Christian worship. Recognising that music should help to renew the mind rather than the emotions it is believed that music and songs must be related to the worship and the Word … We call upon our congregations to give a high priority to improving the standard of Church music, offering possibilities for wider training and experience to organists, choirs and others involved in congregational music. We call on all our people to put new heart into their singing and to let the inspiration and joy of Christian praise be heard in all our Churches."

Coleraine Declaration 1990

IN A GROUP

1. "The playing of instruments other than the organ is disrespectful in church services." Do you agree or disagree? Give reasons for your answer.

2. Do you think certain styles of music exclude some people from participating in worship in a church service? Explain your answer.

ORDERS OF SERVICE

TEACHER'S NOTE

For this section, those studying module 3.1 'The Christian Church through a study of the Catholic Church and One Protestant Tradition' should study the material on the Catholic Church and select one Protestant denomination.

Those studying module 3.2a 'The Christian Church with a focus on the Catholic Church' should study the material on the Catholic Church only.

Those studying module 3.2b 'The Christian Church with a focus on the Protestant Tradition' should study material on one Protestant denomination.
(Continue reading from page 48.)

THE MASS IN THE CATHOLIC CHURCH

In the Catholic Church 'the Mass' is the name given to the celebration of the Eucharist. It is the central act of worship.

THE GREETING AND THE PENITENTIAL RITE

The priest welcomes the people and if appropriate says a few words about the theme of the Mass. For example, the Mass may be in honour of a particular saint or it may be a Mass for the sick. The **Penitential Rite** is important because the congregation acknowledge that they are sorry for their sins and ask God's forgiveness.

THE LITURGY OF THE WORD

This part of the Mass is made up of:

- **The Opening Prayer**
  If the Mass is being said on a Sunday or a feast day then the 'Gloria' is said in worship, praise and thanks.

'Gloria'

"Glory to God in the highest, and peace to His people on earth. Lord God heavenly King, almighty God and Father, we worship you, we give you thanks, we praise you for your glory. Lord Jesus Christ, only Son of the Father, Lord God, Lamb of God, you take away the sin of the world; have mercy on us; you are seated at the right hand of the Father; receive our prayer. For you alone are the Holy One, you alone are the Lord, you alone are the Most High, Jesus Christ, with the Holy Spirit, in the glory of God the Father. Amen."

- **Readings from the Bible**
  One is usually from the Old Testament and one from the New. These are usually read by members of the congregation (the laity). There is also a reading from the Gospel, which is read by the priest.

- **The Homily**
  Here the priest explains the meaning of the readings and helps the congregation to apply it to their everyday lives.

THE CREED AND PRAYERS OF THE FAITHFUL

A creed is a profession of faith said by everyone present. The Mass usually features the **Nicene Creed**. There are also around five **Prayers of the Faithful** or 'Bidding Prayers' in which the people pray for those in need in the Church, the world and the local community.

OFFERTORY

There is usually a procession in which the bread and wine are brought to the altar. Other gifts may be brought as well, such as money donated by the congregation. The priest says a prayer of blessing over the bread and wine and the people say:

"May the Lord accept the sacrifice at your hands, for the praise and glory of his name, for our good, and the good of all his Church."

EUCHARISTIC PRAYERS

The Eucharistic Prayer is made up of the following:

The Preface or introduction, which includes a prayer of thanksgiving and ends with a prayer of praise and thanksgiving, sometimes called the *Sanctus*.

The Consecration of the bread and wine lie at the very heart of the Eucharistic Prayer. The priest repeats the words which Jesus used at the Last Supper: *"This is my body ... this is my blood"* (Matthew 14:22–24). Catholics believe that the bread and wine then become the body and blood of Jesus.

The Proclamation of the Mystery of Faith follows the Consecration. All the people repeat or sing one of these responses:

"Christ has died, Christ is risen, Christ will come again.

"Dying you destroyed our death, rising you restored our life. Lord Jesus, come in glory.

"When we eat this bread and drink this cup, we proclaim your death, Lord Jesus, until you come in glory.

"Lord, by your cross and Resurrection, you have set us free. You are the Saviour of the World."

The Memorial prayer which includes a prayer for the dead, a prayer for the needs of the Church, a prayer to honour the saints of the Church (perhaps the patron saint of that parish church) and a prayer asking for God's blessing on the Church.

The Concluding Doxology, which is a solemn prayer said or sung by the priest.

THE COMMUNION RITE

In this section, members recite the **'Our Father'** prayer and symbolically shake hands with one another as a **sign of peace**. The **Lamb of God** prayer emphasises the Catholic understanding of the death of Jesus as a sacrifice which takes away sin.

The priest then receives the bread and wine and the people walk in procession to the Altar to receive the bread. The Priest holds up the host to each person as they approach him and says the words **"The Body of Christ"** to which the person receiving replies **"Amen"**.

Did you know?

In the Catholic Church, Eucharist bread, like a round wafer, is referred to as 'The Host'. Usually, the people only receive the bread at Mass, though sometimes both bread and wine are given.

CONCLUDING RITE

The priest says a final blessing over the people; **"Go in peace to love and serve the Lord".** The Mass usually ends with a hymn.

When I go to Mass I feel it centres me and reminds me of who I am. I feel a sense of identity and belonging. I come away feeling strengthened and re-energised; ready to start a new week, mindful of what my real priorities in life are. For me there is something really spiritually nourishing about receiving the Body of Christ in Communion and the command to 'go out to love and serve the Lord' reminds me what the focus and purpose of my week at work and at home with my family should really be.

CHURCH OF IRELAND ORDER OF SERVICE

Worship in the Church of Ireland follows the liturgical style – a set structure of words led by one person, but involving the whole congregation. The congregation follows the order of service in **The Book of Common Prayer** or another book.

Most Sunday mornings will feature a Service of Communion (always led by a minister) and a Service of Morning Prayer which can be led by a member of the congregation (a 'lay reader').

The order of service for the Morning Prayer service is outlined below:

GREETING, WELCOME AND HYMN OF PRAISE

The rector will welcome the congregation and invite them to worship God.

MINISTRY OF THE WORD

This includes:

- **Readings**
  Readings from the Old and New Testaments. These readings follow the pattern set out in the *lectionary* – a book which states what passages of scripture should be read each week. A lectionary has a cycle of either two or three years so that the majority of the Bible is read over a period of time.

- **Canticles**
  These are scripture passages set to music.

- **The Apostles' Creed**
  All members of the congregation participate by reciting the Apostles' Creed – a statement of belief.

PRAYERS

Prayer forms an important part of the worship service. People pray standing, sitting or kneeling. *The Revised Catechism of the Church of Ireland* states:

> "Prayer is the uplifting of heart and mind to God. We adore him, we confess our sins and ask to be forgiven, we thank him, we pray for others and for ourselves, we listen to him and seek to know his will."

Written, liturgical prayers, such as the Lord's Prayer, are important in a Church of Ireland service.

There are three main types of prayer used:

1. **Collects,** which are short prayers with three parts.

Collects	
Addressing God	"O God, the author of peace and lover of concord, to know you is eternal life, and to serve you is perfect freedom;
A petition	"'Defend us in all assaults of our enemies, that we, surely trusting in your protection, may not fear the power of any adversaries;
Asking to be heard through Christ	"through Jesus Christ our Lord."

2. **Prayers of confession** (saying sorry for sin);
prayers of intercession (praying for others);
prayers of thanksgiving and **prayers of praise**.

3. **Private prayer.**

HYMNS

Hymns of praise are sung at intervals throughout the service. Depending on the congregation, these could be traditional hymns or modern worship songs, led by a band or the organist and choir.

SERMON

A talk based on the Bible readings. The minister explores the Bible text and its meaning for people's lives.

OFFERING

The congregation give offerings of money, collected in plates or bags. The money is dedicated to the work of God, as a symbol of each person dedicating their whole lives to God. The money pays for the church building and for the various church organisations. Some is given to charities.

BENEDICTION

After a closing hymn the minister gives a word of blessing, such as "Go in peace to love and serve the Lord." The congregation then leave.

❝ I go to the Church of Ireland. I like that it follows a set liturgy because I know exactly what is going to happen next. I like that I don't just sit in my seat and there are times when we all stand or kneel. I really feel part of a community in my church when everyone says the creed or a prayer together. There is also a great feeling of respect in my church. I like the grand surroundings and I think the layout of my church helps me to show reverence to God. **❞**

BAPTIST CHURCH ORDER OF SERVICE

Each individual Baptist congregation decides on its own format for worship services on Sunday morning, but most services follow an order similar to this:

WELCOME AND ANNOUNCEMENTS

The pastor welcomes everyone to the service, particularly newcomers. Any announcements about events in the life of the church are made.

PRAYER

Different types of prayer will be used throughout the service. This first prayer is likely to be a prayer of adoration, focusing the congregation on God. The service will also include prayers of intercession.

The pastor prays in his own words, and may invite a member of the congregation to lead prayer.

HYMNS

Hymns of praise are sung at intervals throughout the service. Depending on the congregation, these could be traditional hymns or modern worship songs.

CHILDREN'S TALK

A talk for the children given by the pastor or another member of the congregation. Normally, children move to the front of the church and the speaker will talk to them face to face. This is sometimes followed by a children's song. After this, the children leave the main service and go to Sunday School or Children's church.

BIBLE READINGS

Parts of the Bible are read by members of the congregation. Many people follow the reading in their own Bibles.

The Bible is of central importance in a Baptist service. The Baptist confession of Faith states that:

> "The Holy Scripture is the only sufficient, certain and infallible rule of all saving knowledge, faith and obedience."

SERMON

A talk based on the Bible readings. The minister explores the Bible text and its meaning for people's lives. This will be the longest part of a Baptist service. Baptists believe they are listening to God through the readings and the words of the speaker.

OFFERING

The congregation give offerings of money, collected in plates or bags. The money is dedicated to the work of God, as a symbol of each person dedicating their whole lives to God.

The money pays for the church building and for the various church organisations. Some is given to charities.

COMMUNION

After a time of quietness and reflection the Pastor invites those gathered to share in communion. Members of the congregation choose a song or hymn. There may also be a spontaneous prayer or Bible reading. The bread and wine are passed out to everyone in their seats. Everyone eats the bread at the same time, followed by the wine.

BENEDICTION

The pastor gives a word of blessing, such as "Go in peace to love and serve the Lord." The congregation then leave.

❝ I go to my local Baptist Church every Sunday. The atmosphere is very relaxed and informal. My favourite part is the time of informal singing before communion where I sometimes get the chance to suggest one of my favourite choruses. Our pastor is a great preacher too and applies the Bible to everyday life. **❞**

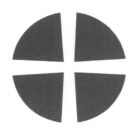

METHODIST CHURCH ORDER OF SERVICE

The style of Methodist worship services varies from congregation to congregation. Some will follow a structured liturgy from the Methodist Service Book, but most will vary their worship from one week to the next.

Most Methodist churches celebrate communion once a month, usually following a set liturgy.

Services generally follow an order similar to this:

PREPARATION

Call to worship

Usually with words from scripture, the minister invites the congregation to worship God.

Hymns

Hymns of praise are sung at intervals throughout the service. Depending on the congregation, these could be traditional hymns or modern worship songs. The Methodist Church has a rich tradition of hymns written by Charles Wesley, one of the Church's founders.

Prayers

The Methodist Catechism gives six different forms of prayer (adoration, confession, meditation, thanksgiving, intercession and petition), all of which may be used throughout the service. **The Lord's Prayer** may also be recited. Set, written prayers are not normally used.

At this point of the service there will usually be prayers of adoration and confession.

MINISTRY OF THE WORD

Hymn

Another hymn is sung to prepare the people to hear God's word.

Children's address

A talk for the children given by the minister or another member of the congregation. Normally, children move to the front of the church and the speaker will talk to them face to face. This is sometimes followed by a children's song. After this, the children leave the main service and go to Sunday School or Children's church.

Bible readings

Parts of the Bible are read by members of the congregation. Many people follow the reading in their own Bibles.

The Bible plays an important part in the worship of the Methodist Church, symbolised by an open Bible placed on the communion table.

> Some Methodist churches base their readings on a lectionary – a cycle of readings from Old and New Testament which ensure the whole Bible is read over the course of a year or more.

Sermon

A talk based on the Bible readings. The minister explores the Bible text and its meaning for people's lives.

RESPONSE

Prayers of meditation and thanksgiving

In some Methodist services there will be a time of quiet for the congregation to reflect on what they have heard. This is a chance to thank God for his message and for all that he has done.

Offering

The congregation give offerings of money, collected in plates or bags. The money is dedicated to the work of God, as a symbol of each person dedicating their whole lives to God.

The money pays for the church building and for the various church organisations. Some is given to charities.

Prayers of Intercession and Petition

The people pray for the needs of others and for themselves.

Hymn

A final hymn of praise to God.

The Grace

The congregation share words of blessing with one another:

> "The grace of the Lord Jesus Christ, the love of God, and the fellowship of the Holy Spirit be with you all" (2 Corinthians 13:13).

"" I love our Sunday morning service. Worshipping through music is very important to me. There is a big focus on community, and it's great to gather and worship God together. ""

PRESBYTERIAN CHURCH: ORDER OF SERVICE

Presbyterian churches celebrate communion between two and six times a year, usually around special festivals.

The style of Presbyterian worship services varies from congregation to congregation. Most contain the same elements of praise, prayer, readings and sermon outlined below:

APPROACH TO GOD

Call to worship

Usually with words from scripture, the minister invites the congregation to worship God.

Hymn or Psalm

Hymns of praise are sung at intervals throughout the service. Depending on the congregation, these could be traditional hymns or modern worship songs. The Presbyterian Church also has a tradition of singing psalms – songs found in the Old Testament which have been set to music.

Prayers of confession

Different types of prayer will be used throughout the service. Set, written prayers are not normally used.

This first prayer is likely to be a prayer of confession, asking God for forgiveness.

Children's address

A talk for the children given by the minister or another member of the congregation. Normally, children move to the front of the church and the speaker will talk to them face to face. This is sometimes followed by a children's song. After this, the children leave the main service and go to Sunday School or Children's church.

Hymn or Psalm

PROCLAMATION OF THE WORD

Bible readings

Parts of the Bible are read by members of the congregation. The Bible is central to Presbyterian worship. An open Bible is placed in the pulpit at the start of each service as a symbol that the congregation is now about to listen to the Word of God. There will be readings from the Old Testament and the New Testament.

Prayers of adoration and praise

These prayers give glory to God and prepare the congregation to hear the word of God.

Sermon

A talk based on the Bible readings. The minister explores the Bible text and its meaning for people's lives. This is the longest part of the service (between 20–30 minutes long).

RESPONSE TO THE WORD

Offering

The congregation give offerings of money, collected in plates or bags. The money is dedicated to the work of God, as a symbol of each person dedicating their whole lives to God.

The money pays for the church building and for the various church organisations. Some is given to charities.

Prayers of intercession

The minister leads people in prayer for the needs of others and for themselves.

Hymn or Psalm

A final song of praise is offered to God.

Blessing and dismissal

A word of blessing is given, such as "Go in peace to love and serve the Lord." The congregation then leave.

" Sunday worship gives me a chance to share in fellowship with others. I like the variety in the Presbyterian Church. It is both modern and traditional and appeals to all age groups. My favourite part is the sermon. I look forward to what the minister has to say. His sermons are really interesting and challenge me to focus on living out my Christian life. "

FOR YOUR FOLDER

1. Describe the normal Sunday act of worship in a denomination of your choice.

2. Why do most church services include a sermon or homily?

3. "Some churches place too much emphasis on preaching. This should not be the main focus of a service of worship." Do you agree or disagree? Give reasons for your answer.

4. Do you think it is a good idea to have the same order of service every Sunday?

5. "Church services are too long and too boring". How might you persuade a teenager who doesn't go to church that this is a false statement?

IN A GROUP

1. There has been an overall decline in the number of people attending church services in Northern Ireland. Why do you think this has happened?

2. Design an order of service that would appeal to your age group. Decide how long the service should be and what should be included.

FELLOWSHIP MEETINGS

As well as meeting on a Sunday for worship services, many Christians meet during the week at smaller and more personal gatherings called fellowship meetings. These meetings may be specifically for prayer or Bible study. Groups can be made up of men and women with a mixture of singles, married couples and families. Other groups are more specific, appealing to men only or women only, to mothers with small children, to teenagers, or to children.

Being a member of a fellowship group means being committed to the others in that group.

- Caring for and looking out for one another.
- Building relationships that are based on trust, openness and honesty.
- Sharing in each other's lives.
- Having fun together.

" Christianity is a lifelong, developing relationship with Jesus. Fellowship meetings, such as Bible study groups, are a place where new Christians can begin to grow in their faith and can ask questions without feeling intimidated. A Bible study group also helps new members to get to know other church members so that they don't feel left out on a Sunday morning. It's always good to see a friendly face in the crowd, especially if there is a large congregation at your church. All Church members can mature and grow in their faith, and learn to depend on one another. Then at the weekend everyone comes together for celebration at the Sunday worship service and it feels like one big family! "

IN A GROUP

"If Christians are so busy meeting together in small groups then they are not fulfilling Christ's command to go into the world" Do you agree or disagree? Explain your answer showing that you have considered more than one point of view.

THE AUTHORITY OF THE BIBLE

Christians believe that the Bible is the Word of God and contains important teachings for believers. There are different views on the authority of the Bible.

Fundamentalist	Moderate	Liberal

1. Fundamentalist
Fundamentalists believe that everything in the Bible is literally true. The Virgin Birth, the miracles of Jesus and the Resurrection are all historical facts. Significantly, they believe that the creation story in Genesis is a literal account of the beginning of the universe and human life. The Bible is the exact word of God and contains no errors.

2. Moderate
Moderates do not consider everything in the Bible literally true. Some of the writings may be explained symbolically rather than factually. It is their meaning today that is important. The writings in the Bible were inspired by God.

3. Liberal
Liberals do not believe that the Bible is the literal Word of God. It is subject to the human error of writers and translators. It may contain truth, but it is not necessary to believe that all the stories are literally true. Some of the teachings of the Bible are a valuable guide for life and the stories may contain themes that are important today.

How is the Bible used by the different denominations?

- In the Protestant denominations the Bible takes central stage. Worship services are based around the Bible. Leaders carefully select which part of the Bible is to be read and studied, and the sermon is based on those readings.

- In some denominations the sermon can last up to 40 minutes but is usually about 20 minutes long. Other parts of the services are also based on the Bible, for example, the reciting of the Lord's Prayer or the singing of Psalms.

- In the Catholic Church, while Bible readings are very important, the main focus is on the Eucharist. There are three Bible readings, one from the Old Testament, one from the Gospels, and one from the rest of the New Testament. A Psalm is also read during the Mass. The priest will give a homily – a short talk based on the readings, helping people to understand the implications for their lives.

- Some Christians like to meet with others to study the Bible. Usually, one person will prepare a topic and lead a discussion for those gathered.

BIBLE READING AIDS

Many Christians read the Bible daily to help them to develop their faith. Some people will take time to read the Bible before they go to school or work, or the end of the day, before they go to sleep. This is usually accompanied by prayer, and many Christians value this time as a chance to communicate with God and listen to what he is saying to them.

Bible reading aids are books designed to help Christians to understand the Bible. Some are aimed to suit specific age groups, which are reflected by the activities outlined in the aid. For example, a Bible reading aid for 7–11 year olds might include word games, puzzles, riddles, cartoons, competitions, simple prayers and daily Bible readings. Reading aids for teenagers are packed with graphics and special features on particular issues which concern teenagers. Most contain daily Bible readings and an explanation of what the readings mean.

The Bible is a very big book and some parts of it are easier to read and understand than others. Some Bible reading aids are designed to take the reader through the whole Bible. This may involve a daily reading schedule, designed to make it easy to read the Bible, for example, in a year.

❝I used to find reading the Bible quite difficult until I found a translation of the Bible which I could understand easily. I try to read the Bible every night. I would often use a devotional book or reading notes. These guide you through a Bible book or a theme and are really helpful.❞

Rachel

❝Reading and studying our Bible is a means by which we can encounter God. I believe it is vital to seek the Lord, and want to know his will. I find that using Bible reading notes each day as part of my quiet time helps to focus my attention on discovering God's will for my life. It also helps me to apply the truth of the Bible to tackling the tough issues in life, to guide me better to hear God's voice through Scripture and prayer, and to encourage me in the struggles that I face.❞

IN A GROUP

Why do you think Rachel likes to read the Bible every day? What benefit does the use of a Bible reading aid have for Rachel?

FOR YOUR FOLDER

Do you think it is important for Christians to read the Bible often? Give reasons for your answer.

THE BIBLE IN THE CATHOLIC TRADITION

"This sacred Synod earnestly and specifically urges all the Christian faithful … to learn by frequent reading of divine Scriptures the excelling knowledge of Jesus Christ … For ignorance of the Scripture is ignorance of Christ."

Dogmatic Constitution on Divine Revelation, Section 25

The Bible is very important in the Catholic Church for a number of reasons:

1. It is the inspired Word of God

The Catholic Church believes that both the Old and the New Testament are the inspired Word of God.

2. It contains important teaching for believers

The Church teaches that the Scripture contains teaching which is 'without error' (Dogmatic Constitution on Divine Revelation, Section 11).

3. It is spiritual food

Jesus said, *"Man cannot live by bread alone but by every word that comes from the mouth of God"* (Matthew 4:4).

4. It challenges Christians to spread the Good News of Salvation

In Mark 16:15–16 Jesus said, *"Go into the whole world and preach the Gospel to the whole of Creation. He who believes and is baptised will be saved, but he who does not believe will be condemned."* Therefore the Catholic Church believes that one of the most important duties of a priest is to proclaim the Gospel.

5. The Scriptures are a way of developing a personal relationship with God

The Church teaches that Christians should read the Bible often so that they can come to know God.

In the Eucharist service there are three Bible readings, one from the Old Testament, one from the Gospels, and one from the rest of the New Testament. A Psalm is also read during the Mass. The priest will give a homily – a short talk based on the readings, helping people to understand the implications for their lives.

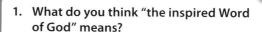

FOR YOUR FOLDER

1. What do you think "the inspired Word of God" means?

2. Explain why the Bible is important to Catholics.

THE IMPORTANCE OF PREACHING

Preaching is a central part of the worship service in some denominations, such as the Baptist Church, the Methodist Church and the Presbyterian Church. Christians believe that one of the ways that God communicates his word to Christians is through preaching. They see the Bible as the Word of God, and believe that the minister or pastor may be inspired by the Holy Spirit when preaching. The sermon is teaching based on the Bible, and it gives listeners a key to understanding and interpreting the Bible. Through the sermon Christians can learn how to apply Biblical teaching to their everyday lives. Bible readings throughout the service are based on the same theme as the sermon.

The minister or pastor will spend time during the week preparing for the sermon, through prayer and study. In some denominations the sermon will be the longest part of the service, lasting between 20 and 40 minutes.

In the Methodist Church both lay (ordinary members) and ordained (ministers) people can preach. In other denominations only the minister will preach, or there may be visiting ministers from another church invited to preach.

Sometimes a sermon will be aimed at those who are not Christians. People find themselves at church for all kinds of reasons, and the sermon is seen as an opportunity to explain the Gospel to them. On other occasions the sermon might be to people who are already Christians, so the focus will be on developing and deepening their faith.
The importance attached to preaching is summed up in the words of the Presbyterian Church:

"Biblical preaching must be at the very heart of true worship. It must, of course, be presented attractively, and applied sharply to the actual situations and needs of our time."

The Coleraine Declaration, 1990

FOR YOUR FOLDER

1. Do you think that it is difficult to accept the literal truth of the Bible in the twenty-first century?
2. What do you think "the Inspired Word of God" means?
3. Explain how the Bible is used in the worship service of a denomination of your choice.
4. How might daily reading of the Bible be a useful exercise for Christians today?
5. Explain why preaching is an important part of the worship of some denominations.
6. Do you think the sermon should be used to comment on moral or political issues?
7. "If churches place too much emphasis on preaching, it makes their services long and boring." Do you agree or disagree? Give reasons for your answer.

 ## MARY AND THE SAINTS

MARY THE MOTHER OF GOD

Mary has a very special position of honour in the Catholic Church. Catholics do not worship Mary, but she is venerated as the Mother of God.

IN A GROUP

Look up the following verses on your own:
Luke 1:26–38　Luke 2: 41–51
John 19: 25–27　Luke 1:39–45
John 2: 1–11

Discuss what qualities Mary shows in these stories. Make a list of your groups findings. Select a few quotations that illustrate these qualities.

What do you think Christians today can learn from the example of Mary?

Catholics honour Mary for a number of reasons:

The Annunciation

Mary played a very special role in working with God to bring about the salvation of humankind because God chose her to be the Mother of the Saviour. This role is the highest honour and dignity that could be given to any human being.

Obedience

None of this would have happened if Mary had not been obedient to what was asked of her. She accepted God's wishes and plans for her at great personal cost. In this way Mary is a perfect role model for Christians of both Christian discipleship and service.

The Immaculate Conception

Because of the special role Mary was to have in the salvation of the world and as the Mother God, Catholics believe that Mary herself was conceived without the ability to sin because she was already chosen by God when she was born.

Virgin mother

Catholics also honour Mary because it was from her that Jesus took his humanity. Luke's Gospel tells us that when the angel visits her, Mary wonders how it is that she will have a baby because she is virgin and not yet married. She is told that she will conceive by the power of the Holy Spirit. Because Jesus was born of the human Mary, he is truly human.

A symbol of the Church

- Just as the angel asked Mary to bring Christ into the world, all are asked the same question. In this way Mary is a representative and symbol of what all Christians should be. She was an ordinary woman, but she said an extraordinary 'yes' to God.

- When on the cross, Jesus gave Mary to John to care for as if she were his mother. Similarly, he gave her to the whole Church as Mother (John 19: 26–27). Because of this Catholics turn to Mary in times of difficulty and pray for her intercession on their behalf.

- As Mary stood at the foot of the cross, she remained faithful to her son at the most difficult time of his life. Christians too are asked to remain faithful to Christ even in most difficult times and to have faith like Mary's.

The Catholic Church has many Feast days in honour of Mary:

8 December	The Immaculate Conception
1 January	Feast of Mary Mother of God
25 March	The Annunciation
31 May	The Visitation of the Blessed Virgin Mary
15 August	The Assumption of the Blessed Virgin Mary
15 September	Our Lady of Sorrows

FOR YOUR FOLDER

Choose any two of the Feast Days and explain what event you think is being remembered and why it is important to the Church.

THE ROLE OF THE SAINTS IN THE CATHOLIC CHURCH

The saints are people who have followed Jesus and lived their lives according to his teaching. Because they are good and virtuous people the Catholic Church believes that they are excellent role models of faith to all Christians. The Catholic Church also teaches that, because of their holiness, the saints have already entered heaven and because of their special closeness to God, many Catholics ask saints to intercede or pray for them.

The saints are not worshipped. Worship is for God alone, and Catholics pray directly to God. Someone asking a saint to pray on their behalf is not very different from asking a friend to pray for you.

Patron Saints

Many churches, schools and hospitals are dedicated to a particular saint. Usually the saint has some connection with that place, for example, there are two churches dedicated to Saint Patrick in Armagh.

NOTE

There is more information on patron saints and saint's days on pages 64, 92–93.

Relics

The Catholic Church especially are interested in the relics of the saint. Anything that was associated with them in life, be it their clothes, objects they have had contact with, or their bones are seen as important and holy. They are preserved and protected and are sometimes objects of devotion.

The chains of St Peter are kept in Rome.

Becoming a saint

The Catholic Church has an official list of saints called the **canon of saints**. There are very strict rules and procedures to follow before someone can be added to the canon. The process of being declared a saint is called **canonisation**. It is a long process involving a thorough and extensive investigation into the person's life to gather evidence of their holiness in life and death. The process itself will not

make someone a saint; it will only declare that they were a saint. The process follows the steps below:

Usually, the bishop of the diocese where the saint lived or died or is buried begins an investigation. It may not start sooner than 5 years after the death of the person being investigated. Eyewitness accounts are gathered and any of the person's writings are read in-depth.

At this stage, the person is referred to as **'Servant of God'**.

The body of the 'Servant of God' is exhumed and any relics are collected.

Evidence is gathered that the 'Servant of God' lived a life of virtue – that they had faith, hope, charity, justice and wisdom beyond what would be expected of an ordinarily 'good' person.

The Pope will declare that the 'Servant of God' has shown that they were 'heroic in virtue' and give them the title **'Venerable'**.

The next stage is called **beatification**. For the 'Venerable' person to be beatified it must be shown that a miracle has occurred because of their intercession. This indicates that they are now in heaven. They are then given the title **'Blessèd'**.

If a second miracle because of prayers of the 'Blessèd' person is verified, then they are given the title 'Saint'. The Church will mark their life with a feast day.

IN A GROUP

1. Why do you think there are such lengthy investigations into someone's life before they can be declared a saint?

2. Why do you think that miracles are required before someone can be declared saint?

3. Read the article on page 60:
In the case of Mother Teresa both Pope John Paul II and Pope Benedict XVI waived the five year period after death and began investigation into her life immediately. Why do you think this is?

IN A GROUP

MIRACLE DECISION SPEEDS UP MOTHER TERESA'S SAINTHOOD

The Pope put Mother Teresa of Calcutta on a fast track to sainthood by approving a miracle attributed to her posthumous intervention yesterday. The move paves the way for Mother Teresa to be beatified, the penultimate step to sainthood.

Vatican officials said Mother Teresa was almost certain to be beatified next autumn to coincide with the 25th anniversary of the Pope's election in 1978.

Mother Teresa died in September 1997 at 87, by which time many Roman Catholics — including the Pope — already regarded her as a saint.

Supporters of her canonisation petitioned the Pope to speed up the rules for the process of beatification, which cannot normally begin until five years after the death of the candidate. The Pope granted an exception in 1999.

For beatification, the Vatican requires proof of at least one miracle attributed to prayers of intercession to the candidate, usually a medically inexplicable recovery from terminal illness.

The Pope gave his approval yesterday to the "miraculous" cure of Monica Bersa, an Indian woman who was cured of cancer of the stomach after praying to Mother Teresa. Doctors at the hospital where the woman was treated have said that she was cured by normal medical treatment.

Source: Richard Owen, *The Times*, 21 December 2002, http://www.timesonline.co.uk/tol/news/world/article804284.ece?print=yes&randnum=1151003209000

4. "The Church needs saints." Do you agree or disagree? Give reasons for your opinion.

STATUES AND ICONS IN THE CATHOLIC CHURCH

Most Catholic churches have statues and icons. They are visual reminders of a religious truth. Just as the cross is a reminder to all Christians of the suffering of Jesus, so a statue of Mary can be a reminder of Mary the Mother of God. Icons are a particular kind of religious art. The figure portrayed in the icon often has an 'otherworldly' and timeless quality about it, which can lift the mind of the Christian to heavenly things.

The Virgin Mary and Child figurine in a church in Alsace, France

Sometimes churches have statues of the patron saint of that church. These act as a reminder of the life story of that Saint, and Christians can be inspired to follow their example.

Often statues have kneelers beside them which offer the believer a place to pray. Catholics do not pray to the statues or icon. However, because they recognise the holiness of that saint, they ask for them to intercede with God on their behalf.

Our Lady of Vladimir, the Holy Protectress of Russia

Statues and icons may also be used as teaching tools. In the early years of the Christian Church many of the faithful were unable to read and write. Statues and icons were an important way to teach about biblical characters or events in the life of Jesus. Statues and icons remain important teaching aids for children today.

FOR YOUR FOLDER

1. Explain why Catholics honour Mary.

2. What does the Immaculate Conception refer to?

3. What you think Christians today can learn from the example of Mary? Explain your answer.

4. What is a saint?

5. Explain the role of saints in the Catholic Church.

6. What is a patron saint?

DIFFERENT TYPES OF PRAYER AND THEIR PURPOSE IN CHRISTIAN WORSHIP

"Almighty God, our heavenly Father
we have sinned in thought and word and deed,
and in what we have left undone.
We are truly sorry and we humbly repent.
For the sake of your son, Jesus Christ,
have mercy on us and forgive us,
that we may walk in newness of life
To the glory of your name. Amen."

Prayer is a way of communicating with or talking to God. It is in itself an act of faith in God and Christians regard it as a means of deepening and developing their relationship with God. For most Christians, prayer is seen as conversation with God, but for the purpose of worship services prayers are sometimes divided into categories, each with a different purpose.

TYPES OF PRAYER

- **Prayers of Adoration**

  In these prayers the person praying wishes to praise or worship God. For example, the Mass in the Catholic Church includes many of these types of prayer, such as the 'Gloria' and the Eucharistic prayers. In the Protestant tradition the minister may use written prayers or compose their own prayers of adoration.

- **Prayers of Contrition and Confession**

  In these types of prayers people admit their own sinfulness and ask for God's forgiveness for that sin. In the Protestant churches they will form part of the normal worship service. In the Catholic Mass there are prayers of contrition in the **Penitential rite**, when the priest leads the people in the '**Lord have Mercy**' prayer or the '**I Confess**' is said. The **Act of Contrition** is another example of this kind of prayer, which may be said privately or when receiving the **Sacrament of Reconciliation**.

- **Prayers of Petition**

  In these prayers the Christian usually asks God for things that they need. These may be physical or spiritual needs. Students often make prayers of petition when they are doing exams asking for the gift of wisdom, or the perseverance required to study hard. Those who are ill may ask for healing or the strength to bear their suffering. Prayers of petition should also express willingness to accept God's will, whatever the outcome.

- **Prayers of Thanksgiving**

  One formal example of a prayer of thanksgiving is the **Grace before meals.** In the Protestant churches prayers of thanksgiving may be said before the offering is collected. 'Eucharist' means 'thanksgiving' and in the Catholic Church the **Eucharistic Prayer** in the Mass is an example of a prayer of thanksgiving.

- **Prayers of Intercession**

  These are prayers for others, when the Christian prays on another's behalf. These prayers are most commonly said when someone is ill or experiencing a period of difficulty in their life.

  In the Protestant churches the minister may reflect upon a national disaster or a problem in the local community.

  In the Catholic Church, people may pray for a particular saint to **intercede** with God on someone's behalf. There is also a strong tradition of praying for those who have died. The **Prayers of the Faithful** in the Mass are an example of prayers of intercession, but often Christians privately say prayers of intercession for others.

TYPE OF PRAYER	DEFINITION	EXAMPLE
Adoration		
Thanksgiving		
Confession		
Petition		
Intercession		

❝ I always turn to God when I am doing exams. It makes me feel calmer. **❞**

FOR YOUR FOLDER

1. Copy and complete the table above. In the third column give examples of the kinds of words which may be used in each kind of prayer.

2. Which types of prayer do you think are being used by these people?

3. What do the statements on this page tell us about why Christians pray?

❝ I prayed a lot when my mum was ill last year. It helped me to deal with her illness and I felt I was doing something to help her. **❞**

❝ I feel closest to God, when I see my children play happily. I remember to give thanks. **❞**

Hallowed be thy name, Thy kingdom come, Thy will be done on earth as it is in heaven. Give us this day our daily bread

Using Technology for Prayer

The Vatican is endorsing new technology that brings the book of daily prayers used by priests straight onto iPhones. Father Paolo Padrini, an Italian priest developed an iPhone and iPod prayer application to be used for prayer.

The application includes the Breviary prayer book in many languages. Another section includes the prayers of the daily Mass, and a third contains various other prayers.

Monsignor Paul Tighe, secretary of the Vatican's Pontifical Council for Social Communications, praised the new application Monday, saying the Church "is learning to use the new technologies primarily as a tool or as a means of evangelising, as a way of being able to share its own message with the world."

Pope Benedict XVI, a classical music lover who was reportedly given an iPod in 2006, encourages methods of reaching out to young people through new media. During last summer's World Youth Day in Sydney, Australia, he sent out mobile phone text messages citing scripture to thousands of registered pilgrims – signed with the tagline "BXVI."

Source: 'Vatican approves iTunes prayer book', *Telegraph*, 17 December 2008, www.telegraph.co.uk

The 'Our Father' or The Lord's Prayer

Jesus taught this prayer to the first disciples, as a pattern for all prayer. The words of the prayer express some of the main beliefs of Christians. For these reasons it is seen as very important, and some denominations recite the prayer in most services. In the Our Father we can see different types of prayer, such as praise, confession, thanksgiving, petition and intercession.

Our Father	When Jesus prays to God, he uses the word *abba* which means 'daddy'. This teaches Christians that God wants the best for his children and is as approachable as a loving father. God should be approached with respect, reverence and awe.
Hallowed be thy name	God's very name is honoured and holy. It should never be used in a casual way but is to be used in reverence and worship. This highlights the importance of putting God's glory first before personal needs are prayed for. The first section of the prayer is adoration.
Thy Kingdom Come, thy will be done, on earth as it is in heaven	The Bible teaches that when Jesus came to earth as a man, God's Kingdom also arrived. Through these words Jesus urges his followers to pray for God's will to be carried out on earth. The words "Thy will be done" help Christians to accept God's plan for them in life.
Give us this day our daily bread	'Bread', a basic food, represents all that a Christian may need. People do not just need physical food to be well. They also pray that their emotional and spiritual needs are met. These words imply that God will supply this help each day as it is needed. This is a prayer of petition.
Forgive us our trespasses as we forgive others who trespass against us	A prayer of confession. Jesus reminded his followers that only those who were prepared to forgive could ask for forgiveness. This is an important part of being a Christian.
And lead us not into temptation but deliver us from evil	This is a request that Jesus' followers will be able to resist any temptations that they may face. Christians express their faith that Jesus has overcome the power of evil by His death.
For thine is the Kingdom, the power and the glory, for ever and ever. Amen	This statement appears in some Greek manuscripts of the Gospel of Matthew, and is usually only said in the Protestant tradition.

SPECIFIC PRAYERS IN THE CATHOLIC TRADITION

The Catholic Church has some prayers that are unique to their worship:

The Rosary

The Rosary is a very traditional prayer of devotion to Mary in the Catholic Church.

People recite set prayers including the **'Hail Mary'** while meditating on important events from the life of Jesus and his mother. Strings of **prayer beads** are used to count the repetitions of the prayers.

In the past the Rosary was a very helpful prayer for those who were poor and couldn't afford a Bible or for those who couldn't read. It helped them to learn important parts of the story of Jesus.

Novenas

Novenas are a popular form of prayer in the Catholic Church.

- The name comes from the Latin *novem,* meaning 'nine'.

- Novenas are short prayers normally prayed over nine days.

- They are often ways of showing devotion to a particular saint and are prayed around the feast day or in a month dedicated to that saint.

- Novenas are often prayers of petition and request: For example, the St Joseph novena, completed because he is the patron saint of fathers, to ask for the grace and strength to be a good parent; or the St Anthony novena, to find a lost article or possession.

Stations of the Cross

The Stations of the Cross are a series of fourteen images, each representing an event in the last day of Jesus' life. They are a very important devotional exercise in the Catholic Church. People make their way from station to station, pausing at each to pray and to meditate on the suffering of Jesus.

> ### Did you know?
>
> In the early Church it was common for Christians to go the Jerusalem and trace the actual journey Jesus made on his way to Calvary. War in the Middle Ages made this no longer possible and it became popular to complete the prayerful pilgrimage in local churches. This is how the Stations of the Cross originated.

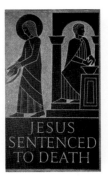

The Stations of the Cross

JESUS SENTENCED TO DEATH

JESUS TAKES UP HIS CROSS

JESUS FALLS THE FIRST TIME

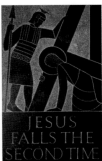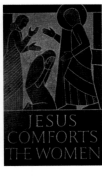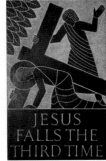

JESUS FALLS THE SECOND TIME

JESUS COMFORTS THE WOMEN

JESUS FALLS THE THIRD TIME

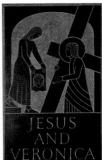

JESUS MEETS HIS MOTHER

JESUS IS HELPED BY SIMON

JESUS AND VERONICA

JESUS IS STRIPPED NAKED

FORGIVE THEM — JESUS NAILED TO THE CROSS

JESUS DIES ON THE CROSS

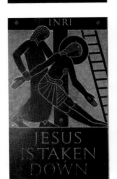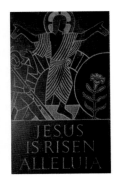

JESUS IS TAKEN DOWN

JESUS IS LAID IN THE TOMB

JESUS IS RISEN ALLELUIA

FOR YOUR FOLDER

1. Name three different types of prayer.
2. What does the 'Our Father' teach about forgiveness?
3. What is a prayer of Contrition?
4. What are the Stations of the Cross?
5. Explain why Novenas are prayed.
6. Describe the different uses of prayer in a church service. You may use examples from more than one denomination.

IN A GROUP

Discuss:

1. Do you think the Stations of the Cross are a useful aid to prayer? Give reasons for your answer.
2. "Repetitive public prayers like the 'Our Father' or Lord's Prayer makes them become meaningless." Do you agree or disagree? Give reasons for your answer.
3. Why do you think different types of prayer are used in church worship?
4. Explain why the 'Our Father' or Lord's Prayer is important to Christians.

Chapter 4

CHURCH ARCHITECTURE AND FURNITURE

If you walk down the street you will pass many different kinds of buildings – houses, offices, businesses and shops. You may be able to guess from looking at them what goes on inside. Church buildings are often very noticeable, with eye-catching architecture or beautiful art displayed in their windows.

The design of most church buildings is filled with symbolism. This means that you can tell a surprising amount about a group of Christians and their beliefs by looking at the building they meet in. The shape, style and size of the building, and even how the furniture is placed on the inside can reveal what is important to that church's members.

For example, if the communion table or altar is in the centre of the church building, then the act of Communion, Mass or Eucharist is probably central in the life of the congregation. If an open Bible, or the **pulpit** where the preacher stands, is in the centre of the church building then the focus of the congregation is probably on the Word of God.

CHURCH ARCHITECTURE

Throughout the UK and Ireland there are church buildings of different shapes and sizes. Even within the same Christian denomination there can be variety, depending on when a church was built, the location of the church and the beliefs of those who worship there. When we look at a church building we can usually work out what is important to its members.

FOR YOUR FOLDER

Think about the different church buildings that are in your town. Try to answer the following questions:

1. Describe the shape of the church buildings.

2. Where are the church buildings situated?

3. Are the buildings new or old? How can you tell?

4. What materials were used to build the church?

5. Do any of the buildings have a tower or a spire?

Church buildings are generally constructed in one of three shapes: the rectangular barn-style, cruciform shape and circular.

Some buildings may have other unique features such as a hall and tower, or be built in a particular way that was popular at the time, such as the Gothic style.

Barn-style

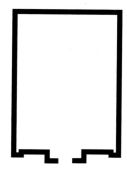

A barn-style church building is shaped like a rectangle. This shape is usually used by denominations that focus on the importance of the Word of God. It is associated with the Presbyterian Church and the Baptist Church. Attention is focused on the front of the room, where the **pulpit** is normally placed in the centre. In some cases, where there is a larger congregation, there is a gallery at the back and sides.

Cruciform

The word 'cruciform' means 'cross-shaped'. Churches use the cruciform shape to highlight the importance of the death of Christ.

The cruciform shape is divided into the following sections:

- The **chancel** at the top of the cross contains the altar, the sanctuary and the choir.

- The **transepts** are the horizontals of the cross shape. They are often used as small chapels.

- The **nave** is the main part of the church where the congregation sits.

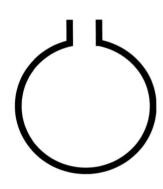

Circular

An increasing number of church buildings are being built in the modern, circular style. Wherever you sit you are able to look directly at other people. This communicates that the people are a Christian fellowship, participating in worship together, rather than simply being spectators. Every member of the church is of equal importance.

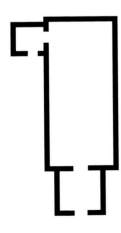

Hall and tower

This is quite similar to the barn-style, but has a tower attached to the rectangular hall. Historically, church buildings were places where people could shelter from attack, which is why some church buildings look more like fortresses. In more modern buildings the tower is symbolic of taking refuge in God: *"The Lord is like a strong tower, where the righteous can go and be safe"* (Proverbs 18:10).

High towers decorated with steeples and spires pointing to the sky are a symbol for the Resurrection. They also make church buildings a notable landmark.

Gothic Style

Gothic architecture originated in France and became popular in the Middle Ages and again in Victorian times.

The Gothic style is associated with high ceilings, pointed arches, large towers and spires. The design points to the mystery, holiness and majesty of God. It is a common style in great churches and cathedrals. The Catholic Cathedral in Armagh is an example of gothic style.

FOR YOUR FOLDER

Copy and complete the following table on the symbolism associated with church architecture:

Shape/Features	Symbolism
Barn-style	
Cruciform	
Circular	
Hall and Tower	
Gothic	

CHURCH FURNITURE

THE CATHOLIC CHURCH

Architecture

Catholic Church buildings can vary in style. Older buildings tend to be built in traditional shapes: cruciform, barn-style, hall and tower, normally made from stone and often in the Gothic style.

More recently some church buildings have been built with more contemporary designs, sometimes circular or oval in shape and generally more simplistic in layout. Many changes in the layout of the church were made as a result of Vatican II (the second Vatican Council).

Sanctuary

The word **sanctuary** means 'sacred' or 'set apart'. In the Catholic Church the sanctuary is an area at the front of the church building which contains the altar, tabernacle and ambo.

In cruciform buildings the sanctuary is situated at the east of the building, symbolizing the Resurrection (the sun rises in the east and the city of Jerusalem, where Jesus died, is also in the east).

To access the sanctuary, the congregation moves from the main body, the nave, and climbs steps, symbolising drawing closer to God.

Did you know?

The second Vatican Council was a meeting of the Catholic Church's hierarchy (leaders), lasting from 11 October 1962 until 8 December 1965. It looked for ways to make the study of scripture and Church teachings more relevant to the current times. It also attempted to address the place of the Catholic Church in terms of the political, social and economic changes of that time.

FURTHER THINKING

How might the sanctuary be compared to the 'Holy of Holies' in the Jerusalem Temple at the time of Jesus?

Altar

The altar is the main focus of the building. It is a table, usually very ornate, made of wood or marble. The table will be draped in a cloth that matches the **liturgical colour** reflecting the seasons of the Church Calendar.

It is at this table that the priest says the words of the Mass service every day, and people come forward to receive the Eucharist. A chalice containing wine and sacred vessels containing bread (the host) are placed on the altar.

> In the Old Testament an altar was a place where a sacrifice was offered, and the Eucharist is a reminder of Christ's sacrifice on the cross.

Catholics believe in **transubstantiation**, which means that the bread and wine become the body and blood of Christ. The congregation forms a queue in front of the altar where the priest gives them a wafer of bread (the body of Christ). Normally only the priest takes the wine (the blood of Christ).

Did you know?

In the past it was common for the altar to be against the front wall of the church which meant that the priest celebrated some parts of the Mass with his back to the congregation.

Since the second Vatican Council, however, a more open approach has been encouraged, with the altar in most churches having been moved closer to the congregation and the priest facing the people throughout the service.

In some churches this has led to the altar being in the centre of the church, creating a sense of fellowship, with the priest being among the people, rather than separate from them.

Tabernacle

The tabernacle is a special receptacle (box) which is situated behind the altar. After Mass the priest places the 'Blessed Sacrament' of bread in the tabernacle. This is a mark of respect for the presence of Christ

in the bread. The bread may later be taken to church members who were unable to attend Mass because of illness.

The tabernacle is also a focus for those who enter the church during the day, perhaps to pray. When the consecrated bread is inside the tabernacle a red light, the sanctuary lamp, is lit to indicate the special presence of Christ. Catholics genuflect (bend their knee) in the direction of the tabernacle as a mark of respect to Christ's presence in the Eucharist inside the tabernacle.

The tabernacle in St Brigid's in Belfast has an image of fish and bread on the front. The fish was used as a symbol by early Christians to indicate their faith in Jesus Christ, Son of God, Saviour (the first letters of which in Greek make up the Greek word for fish). The bread represents the Eucharist.

> At the time of Moses the tabernacle was literally a tent where the presence of God was said to dwell. Since then the word has come to mean any physical place where God is believed to be specially present, such as the bread and wine.

Ambo

The ambo is a reading desk usually situated to the left of the altar. Members of the congregation use the ambo to read the first two scriptural readings in the Mass, and the priest or deacon reads the Gospel

and says the homily from the ambo. This is similar to the **pulpit** in other denominations.

Baptismal Font

The font is a container for the water used in baptism. Sometimes these are ornate pieces of furniture made from stone

or wood, or simply a plain bowl that is brought into the church for baptismal services.

In traditionally shaped buildings the font is situated at the back, close to the main door, symbolising initiation into membership of the Church and the first step taken towards God. In more modern buildings the font may be placed nearer to the altar.

> The Catholic Church performs infant baptism. Through the sacrament of baptism a Christian child belongs to Christ. However, an unbaptised person, who finds faith later in life, can also be baptised into the Catholic Church. Adult baptisms take place at Easter.
>
> Baptism is one of the three *sacraments of initiation* in the Catholic Church. Confirmation and Eucharist are the other two.

THE CHURCH OF IRELAND

Architecture

Most Church of Ireland buildings are built in the traditional cruciform shape. This emphasizes the importance of the cross to Christian beliefs. Some buildings are rectangular, but may appear to be cruciform inside.

Church of Ireland buildings traditionally feature high towers next to the main building. These often contain bells which are rung to call people to worship and to mark particular times of joy and sadness in the community.

Sanctuary

The word **sanctuary** means 'sacred' or 'set apart'. In the Church of Ireland the sanctuary is an area at the front of the church building which contains the Communion table.

In cruciform buildings the sanctuary is situated at the east of the building, symbolising the Resurrection (the sun rises in the east and the city of Jerusalem, where Jesus died, is also in the east).

To access the sanctuary, the congregation moves from the main body, the nave, and climbs steps, symbolising drawing closer to God.

Holy table or Communion table

The Communion table is the main focus of the building. It is usually very ornate, made of wood or marble. The table will be draped in a white linen cloth or one that matches the **liturgical colour** reflecting the

seasons of the Church Calendar.

The bread and wine for communion are set on the table, covered with a white cloth. During the communion service the minister uncovers the bread and wine, and the congregation come forward and kneel around a low rail called the **communion rail**. The minister and others pass out the bread and wine.

> Not unlike the Catholic Church, the positioning of the Communion table has changed since the 1960s. Some churches have moved the communion table down into the main body of the church so that the whole congregation can gather around it as a family. This communicates that God is not distant and remote, but at the heart of the community.

Pulpit

The pulpit is a raised platform and reading desk in one, from which the sermon is given, usually by a minister or deacon. In the Church of Ireland, the pulpit tends to be positioned on the left (north) side of the front of the building.

The pulpit can be made from wood, granite or similar materials, sometimes elaborately carved with Christian symbols or an inscription such as 'Ye are ambassadors for Christ'. The pulpit is also decorated with a piece of fabric, called a **pulpit fall**. The pulpit fall changes to match the **liturgical colour** reflecting the seasons of the Church Calendar.

The pulpit is raised so that the congregation can both see and hear during the sermon, but in some churches the speaker chooses to leave the pulpit and speak from a lectern closer to the congregation, creating a sense of fellowship.

Lectern

The lectern is a reading desk used in the Church of Ireland for scripture readings. It is usually placed on the right (south) side in the sanctuary.

Traditionally, Church of Ireland lecterns are made of brass and shaped like an eagle perched on a globe – its wings outstretched to hold the open Bible. This arrangement is very symbolic.

- The strength and majesty of the eagle shows the importance and strength of the Word of God in the mission of the Church.

- The eagle is also a symbol of St John, the Gospel writer.

- The globe represents the world.

- The outstretched wings represent the Gospel being carried throughout the world.

Font

The font is a container for the water used in baptism. Traditionally these are large, permanent pieces of furniture, often made of ornately carved stone. In cruciform buildings the font is situated at the back, close to the main door, symbolising the first step taken towards God. This part of the building is called the **baptistery**.

Most Church of Ireland buildings now feature a portable font made of wood, with a steel bowl to hold the water. Baptisms take place at the front of the church, symbolising baptism into the community of the church.

THE BAPTIST CHURCH

Architecture

Most Baptist churches are quite plain buildings, simple in design, with a main hall, sometimes a secondary hall and a kitchen. Many are built in residential areas and are therefore designed to fit into the surrounding architecture.

Pulpit

The pulpit is a raised platform and reading desk in one, from which the sermon is given, usually by the pastor or an elder. The pulpit is the most prominent feature in Baptist Church buildings. It is usually made of wood, plainly designed, and positioned on a stage area at the front of the church. The physical centrality of the pulpit symbolises the centrality of the Word of God in the life of the church.

Communion table

This is a simple, wooden table where the bread and wine for communion are kept throughout the service. The table may have an inscription from the Bible, but its simplicity shows that worship does not have to be elaborate or complicated to please God.

It is usually placed in the centre, in front of the pulpit, symbolising that everything, including communion, comes from the Word of God. During the communion service, elders take the bread and wine to the people, who remain seated.

Lectern

The lectern is a reading desk used for scripture readings. It is a small, plain, wooden stand, placed below the pulpit. Some pastors prefer using the lectern instead of the pulpit for the sermon, as it brings them closer to the congregation.

Baptistery

The baptistery is a large, tiled tank, which holds the water for baptism. It is a very important feature in the Baptist Church.

The Baptist Church baptises people as adults by total immersion in water, so a large tank is required. Usually, the baptistery is directly below the communion table and is covered when not in use. There are steps leading down into the baptistery on each side for easy access.

THE METHODIST CHURCH

Architecture

Methodist buildings vary greatly in style and shape depending on when they were built. Often they are simple rectangular halls, but there are also more modern and more traditional designs. No two Methodist church buildings are the same.

The unusual architecture of Dundonald Methodist church.

Communion table

This is a table, usually made of wood, where the bread and wine for communion are set, covered with a white cloth. It is placed in the centre, at the front of the church building. Depending on the individual church the table could be plain or ornately carved or engraved with a phrase from scripture, such as: *"Do this in remembrance of me"*.

During the communion service the minister uncovers the bread and wine, and the congregation come forward and kneel around a low rail called the **communion rail**. The minister and others pass out the bread and wine.

Pulpit

The pulpit is a raised platform and reading desk in one, from which the sermon is given, usually by the minister. The pulpit is usually made from wood and decorated with a piece of fabric called a **pulpit fall**. The pulpit fall can be plain or embroidered with a symbol, such as a dove.

In traditional Methodist buildings the pulpit is high up at the front of the church, behind the communion table. The physical centrality of the pulpit symbolises the centrality of the Word of God in the life of the church.

In more modern buildings, the pulpit is placed to one side, with the focus on the communion table, creating an atmosphere of sharing.

Lectern

The lectern is a reading desk used for scripture readings. It is usually made of plain wood, occasionally decorated with a cross. Some ministers prefer using the lectern instead of the pulpit for the sermon, as it brings them closer to the congregation.

Font

The font is a container for the water used in baptism. In most Methodist church buildings these are portable, carved wooden pieces with a steel bowl to hold the water. Baptisms take place at the front of the church, symbolising baptism into the community of the church.

THE PRESBYTERIAN CHURCH

Architecture

Most Presbyterian churches are built in the rectangular barn-style, often with a gallery. They are usually plain in design, showing that worship does not have to be elaborate or complicated to please God.

Pulpit

The pulpit is a raised platform and reading desk in one, from which the sermon is given, usually by the minister. The pulpit is the most prominent feature in Presbyterian buildings. It is traditionally high up at the front of the church, behind the communion table, emphasising the authority of the Word of God.

The pulpit is usually made from wood and decorated with a piece of fabric called a **pulpit fall**. The pulpit fall is embroidered with the symbol of the Presbyterian Church – a 'burning bush' and the words *Arden Sed Virens*, which means 'burning but flourishing'. This reflects the Presbyterian belief that the Word of God will last forever.

In more modern buildings, the pulpit is placed to one side, with equal focus on the font and communion table.

Communion Table

This is a wooden table from which communion is served between two and six times every year. Depending on the individual church the table could be plain or ornately carved or engraved with a phrase from scripture, such as: *"Do this in remembrance of me"*.

The communion tables is usually placed in the centre, in front of the pulpit, emphasising the Presbyterian belief that the act of communion takes second place to the word of God. During the communion service, elders take the bread and wine to the people, who remain seated.

Lectern

The lectern is a reading desk used for scripture readings. It is usually made of plain wood, occasionally decorated with a cross. Some ministers prefer using the lectern instead of the pulpit for the sermon, as it brings them closer to the congregation.

Font

The font is a container for the water used in baptism. In most Presbyterian church buildings these are portable, carved wooden pieces with a steel bowl to hold the water. Some churches have larger, permanent fonts and others have no font, simply placing a glass bowl on the communion table for baptism.

The font is placed at the front of the church, below the pulpit. This signifies that even baptism takes second place to the Word of God.

FOR YOUR FOLDER

1. Describe the location and function of the main furnishings in a church building of your choice. Some of the pieces you choose may include:
   • Lectern
   • Altar/communion table
   • Pulpit
   • Stations of the cross
   • Tabernacle
   • Font

2. Using relevant examples explain why there are sometimes differences in the architecture and layout of church buildings. For example, explain why some churches are plain inside while others are more decorative.

3. "Christians can worship God properly only in a church building." Do you agree or disagree? Give reasons for your answer.

4. "Ornate and decorative church buildings are a distraction for worshippers." Do you agree or disagree? Give reasons for your answer.

IN A GROUP

1. "Churches could make better use of their buildings to serve the whole community". Do you agree or disagree? Give reasons for your answer showing that you have considered different points of view.

2. "The content of worship rather than the place of worship is what really matters." Do you agree or disagree? Give reasons for your answer showing you have considered more than one point of view.

Chapter 5

CHURCH FESTIVALS

Throughout history people have marked the passing of the seasons with celebrations, rituals and times of feasting and fasting. You may look forward to Christmas and summer holidays as markers in your year. No matter what your background, you probably have annual traditions that you enjoy during the winter holiday. These traditions give a sense of rhythm to our lives, and allow us time to rest and reflect, to celebrate and enjoy ourselves.

Every religion marks significant episodes in the lives of key people. Most Christian festivals remember an important event in the life of Christ. Others may focus on the life of a special person, for example, Saints' Days. Whatever the festival, each is a time for Christians to reflect on their own personal faith.

Just as the school year begins in September, the Christian Church has its own 'Liturgical Calendar', which begins with the season of Advent at the end of November.

Festivals and holidays have almost always held a religious significance for people – literally 'Holy Days'. Before the birth and spread of Christianity in the western world, the year was marked by pagan festivals. For example, the 25 December was originally associated with the pagan 'Birthday of the Sun', marking the beginning of longer hours of daylight. As Christianity spread pagan festivals were slowly replaced by Christian festivals.

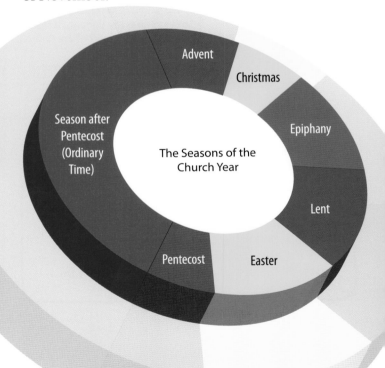

Advent

Christmas

Epiphany

Season after Pentecost (Ordinary Time)

The Seasons of the Church Year

Lent

Pentecost

Easter

FOR YOUR FOLDER

1. Why might some people find following a calendar of the Church year a useful aid to worship?
2. Explain the purpose of celebrating Christian festivals.
3. Look at the table below, which outlines the Christian festivals that fall throughout the year. Copy out the table and describe how each festival is celebrated in a church in your area.

FESTIVAL	PURPOSE	HOW IS IT CELEBRATED?
Advent	To prepare for the coming of Christ	
Christmas	To celebrate the birth of Christ	
Epiphany	To remember the visit of the Magi	
Lent	A time to reflect and prepare for Easter	
Holy Week	To remember the last week of the life of Christ	
Easter Sunday	To celebrate the Resurrection of Christ	
Ascension Sunday	To celebrate the Ascension of Christ	
Pentecost	To remember the coming of the Holy Spirit; the beginning of the Church	
Harvest	A day of thanksgiving for food	

IN A GROUP

You may already have noticed that some Christian festivals fall on the same date every year (for example, Christmas Day), whereas other festivals have a different date every year (for example, Easter Sunday). Can you think of a reason for this?

 ### ADVENT

The word Advent comes from the Latin word *adventus* which means 'coming'. The season of Advent is all about focusing on the coming of Jesus as Messiah and preparing for Christmas. It is a time of waiting and preparation, hope and joy. For many Christians it is a time for focusing on their own hopes, dreams and expectations. Some see Advent as an extension of Christmas, other churches, such as the Catholic Church, see Advent as an important season in itself.

Advent begins four Sundays before Christmas Day and lasts for the next four weeks until Christmas Eve.

HOW DOES THE CHURCH CELEBRATE ADVENT?

Sunday Worship

Each Sunday of the Advent season is marked with special readings from the Bible focusing on the coming of the Messiah, a well as the second coming of Jesus.

> *The Lord himself therefore will give you a sign. It is this: the maiden is with child and will soon give birth to a Son, whom she will call Immanuel*
>
> (Isaiah 7:14)

Liturgical Colour

Different seasons in the Church calendar have different symbols, different traditions and even different colours. These colours will appear in furniture, decoration and clerical clothing.

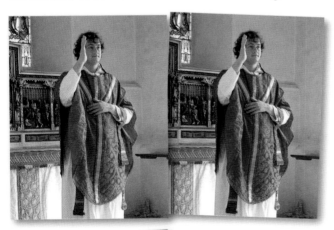

The liturgical colour for Advent is purple. Purple is associated with penance – a time of reflection and turning away from sin. Purple is also associated with royalty, and Advent is a time of preparation for the coming of a king.

Rose pink is the colour for the third week of Advent, representing a move away from the solemn time of penance towards the joy and celebration of Christmas.

Advent Wreath

This custom originated in Germany. A circular wreath of evergreen represents the eternal life of God. It features four candles, symbolising that Christ is the 'Light of the world'. One candle is lit on each Sunday of Advent. There are three purple candles and a fourth pink candle. Some wreaths feature a fifth, white candle at the centre, which is lit on Christmas day.

The Jesse Tree

The Jesse Tree is the family tree of Jesus, tracing his ancestry back to Jesse, the father of King David. It focuses Christians on the humanity of Jesus and reminds them of the importance of the Incarnation.

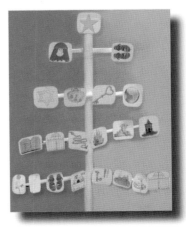

> "*The royal line of David is like a tree that has been cut down; but just as new branches sprout from a stump, so a new king will arise from among David's descendants*" (Isaiah 11:1).

The Christingle

Some churches have a 'Christingle' service on the fourth Sunday of Advent. This is a carol service of Scandinavian origin at which every child receives an orange and candle wrapped in a red ribbon. The candle represents Jesus, the light of the world, and the ribbon stands for the blood of Christ and the love of God embracing the world.

The Advent Calendar

This is a twenty-four day calendar for the month of December. Children can open one window of the calendar each day to reveal a picture or a piece of chocolate. Some families may include a suggestion of a good deed that person can do for someone in their family or neighbourhood.

Advent Resolutions

Just as people make New Year's resolutions, Advent, the beginning of the Church Year, is a time of reflection when people re-evaluate their lives. Many Christians decide on changes they want to make in their own lives and ask God to help them.

> ### Did you know?
>
> Like Lent, Advent is seen in the Catholic Church as a time for quiet and solemn reflection. Some traditionally joyous prayers, such as the 'Gloria' are left out of the Mass during this season. For these reasons, Advent has been called the 'little Lent'.

An example of Advent services in the Church of Ireland

Sunday 7 December – The Second Sunday of Advent

10:00 am Holy Communion

11:00 am Sung Eucharist Communion Service

Sunday 14 December – The Third Sunday of Advent

10:00 am Holy Communion

11:00 am Choral Matins

3:15 pm Sung Eucharist Communion Service

Sunday 21 December – The Fourth Sunday of Advent

10:00 am Holy Communion

11:00 am Sung Eucharist

3:15 pm Festival of Nine Lessons and Carols

Sunday 28 December – The First Sunday of Christmas

10:00 am Holy Communion

11:00 am Said Eucharist

3:15 pm Evening Prayer

FOR YOUR FOLDER

Copy and complete the table below explaining how each Advent custom communicates the meaning of the season of Advent.

Advent Wreath	
Jesse Tree	
Advent calendar	
Advent resolution	

"When I first think of Advent I think of how much I have to do and how many shopping days there are left . I have to get organised to take the children to see Santa and go to all the Christmas parties. I can start to feel quite stressed. Then I go to church and see the purple drapes, the beautiful Jesse tree which the Primary school children made and the Advent wreath on the altar and I feel a sense of peace and hope."

Orla is 35 years old.

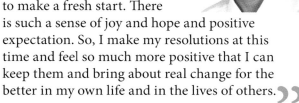

"Because it is the beginning of the Church year I treat Advent as many people do New Year. It is time for me to make a fresh start. There is such a sense of joy and hope and positive expectation. So, I make my resolutions at this time and feel so much more positive that I can keep them and bring about real change for the better in my own life and in the lives of others."

Julia is 70 years old.

"We love Advent. It makes us feel happy and excited. Every day we open a window in the Advent Calendar. We get a little story from the Bible and a picture. Our mummy puts in a sweet as well. In school every Monday we light the candles on the Advent wreath. We can see we are getting closer and closer to Christmas and Jesus' birthday."

Rónán is 8 and Éile is 5.

IN A GROUP

Read the statements to your left and summarise what each person understands about the importance of Advent.

CHRISTMAS

Christmas is the Christian festival that celebrates the birth of Christ. The word 'Christmas' is actually an abbreviation of two words: 'Christ's Mass'. In our society Christmas is celebrated on 25 December. It is a national holiday and most places of work come to a standstill on Christmas Day.

THE ORIGINS OF CHRISTMAS

The story of the birth of Christ is told in two of the four Gospels: Matthew and Luke. Each Gospel adds something different to the story: Matthew mentions the visit of the magi – the wise men, whereas Luke includes the story of the shepherds, and the baby laid in a feeding trough.

Both accounts agree that Jesus' birth was miraculous, that he was conceived by the Holy Spirit and born in Bethlehem to Mary, who was engaged to be married to Joseph.

IN A GROUP

What comes to your mind when you hear the word 'Christmas'? In groups make a list of all the things you associate with Christmas.

CUSTOMS ASSOCIATED WITH CHRISTMAS

From November onwards, it is hard to forget that Christmas is on the way. Town centres are strewn with coloured fairy lights, Christmas trees and artificial snow on shop windows. Shopping centres stay open late and Christmas music seems to be played everywhere you go. By mid-December, most houses are decorated with Christmas trees, coloured lights and decorations.

With all the preparations complete, children go to bed early on Christmas Eve and wait for the morning. Some Christmas day traditions include exchanging and opening presents, Christmas dinner, pulling crackers, visiting family and friends, playing games and watching Christmas television.

> **Did you ever have your picture taken with Santa when you were younger? Why not bring your Santa photos into class?**

FOR YOUR FOLDER

Do Christmas customs add to the true meaning of the Christmas story?

Look at the list of customs associated with Christmas in the table below and find out their origins and what they mean.

In groups discuss each custom and decide if you think it adds to or takes away from the true meaning of Christmas – the story of the birth of Christ.

Christmas Custom	Meaning of custom	Does it add to the true meaning of Christmas?
Christmas cards		
Christmas tree		
Holly		
Mistletoe		
Carol singing		
Nativity play		
Nativity scene		
Santa		
25 December		

HOW IS CHRISTMAS CELEBRATED BY THE CHRISTIAN CHURCH?

Christmas is a very special time in the Church's calendar and there are many ways in which the festival is celebrated. Some denominations, especially those with a strong tradition of singing, hold carol services and children take part in Nativity plays retelling the story of Jesus' birth.

Shrove or Pancake Tuesday

Many of you will be familiar with the term 'Pancake Tuesday'. Supermarkets take the opportunity to advertise batter and lemon juice in the hope of boosting their profits. Families put their frying pans on to see who can flip their pancake the highest. There may even be pancakes sold in your school canteen on this day. But do you know the real meaning behind the day?

Within the Christian Church, Pancake Tuesday is called Shrove Tuesday. During the Middle Ages Christians would go to confession on this day, to be 'shriven'. This simply means that they received forgiveness for their sins. As time went on Shrove Tuesday came to be remembered as the day before the long fast of Lent. It was necessary to use up all the forbidden ingredients such as fat and oil, and so the tradition of making pancakes arose.

In some parts of the world Shrove Tuesday has developed into a day of carnivals and parties. For example, in New Orleans, USA, there is a famous celebration called the *Mardi Gras* (which means 'Fat Tuesday' in French), which consists of parades, street festivals and parties.

Ash Wednesday

The first day of Lent is called Ash Wednesday. In the Middle Ages people wore sackcloth and covered their head in ashes as a sign of penance (being sorry for their sins). In the Catholic Church today people go to a special church service to be 'signed with ashes'. This means that the priest marks the sign of the cross on a person's forehead with ashes. The ash on the forehead shows everyone whom the person meets that they are sorry for their sins and intend to live a better life.

Lent in the Catholic Church

Ash Wednesday is an appropriate beginning to the season of Lent – a period of prayer and fasting in preparation for Easter. Giving to others who are less well off – 'almsgiving' – is another important aspect of Lent for Catholics.

Prayer

Lent is a period of prayer in the Catholic Church. Many Catholics make a commitment to go to Mass every day. For others it means making a point of finding more time each day to focus on God and on developing a relationship with him.

Fasting

This is a voluntary practice, and the extent to which people fast is a matter for the individual. It is a means of focusing on spiritual things rather than material things, and also helps to develop self-control.

Fasting means that Catholics limit the amount that they eat during Lent. For example, some restrict themselves to three meals a day, and so they say they are 'fasting between meals'. Catholics are asked by the Church to 'fast between meals' on Ash Wednesday and Good Friday.

Catholics may also **abstain** from certain foods. For some Catholics this means avoiding meat for all of Lent or, traditionally, on Wednesdays and Fridays.

Most Catholics choose to give up certain foods or hobbies that they find enjoyable as an act of self-sacrifice during Lent.

Today many Catholics practice fasting, not by giving up foods, but by giving up certain habits; for example, gossiping, criticising others or disobeying parents.

Fasting can also be an act of **solidarity** with those who do not have enough to eat.

Almsgiving

66 Going without things does not consist only in giving what we do not need; sometimes it also consists in giving away what we do need. 99

Pope John Paul II

Giving to others is an important part of Lent for Catholics. The Catholic charity Trócaire run an annual Lenten campaign which is supported by many people. Families collect Trócaire money boxes from their local church and return them at the end of Lent. Schools also get involved in fundraising.

TRÓCAIRE

Working for a Just World

"We work for a just world."

"We work with amazing people to bring about positive and lasting changes in some of the world's poorest places."

"Our programmes are carried out with partner organisations so local people drive the whole process and, in turn, their own development."

Source: http://www.trocaire.org/whatwedo

Amoo Gulyemina and her family live in Kilongo, Uganda, after being forced from their family home by conflict. They are pictured with the ox they received from Trócaire's Global Gift Plan. They also received seeds and agricultural training.

Amoo said:

"This gift will make our life easier. We will be able to grow more food and thanks to the ox, we will not have to dig the land by hand. This means we'll be able to plough a larger area and grow more food."

Trócaire 24 Hour Fast

For more than a decade, people have taken part in the Trócaire Fast – a fun and rewarding way to help raise vital funds for developing countries like Uganda. The idea is to stay off food for 24 hours as an act of solidarity with the world's poorest people, and collect sponsorship.

As well as the fast, Trócaire suggest a number of fundraising events including Cake Sales, Car Washing, Coffee Mornings and completing dares.

Source: http://www.trocaire.org/en/Donate

Lent in the Protestant denominations

There is less of a focus on Lent in some of the Protestant denominations than in the Catholic Church, but it is still an important time of reflection and preparation for Easter for many Christians. Some churches celebrate Shrove Tuesday with pancake suppers, and Ash Wednesday and Good Friday are fast days for Anglicans. The forty days of Lent may be marked with special Bible studies focusing on the Easter story or on Jesus' time in the wilderness. There may be special prayer meetings where people can pray together in small groups, or services where the whole church gathers for prayer and meditation.

An example from the Methodist Church: 'Buy Less Live More'

During Lent 2008 the British Methodist Church ran a 'Buy Less, Live More' campaign. Those who took part received an email every day of lent including prayers, readings and two challenges – one to 'Buy Less' (for example, 'Think twice about ordering that unnecessary trinket or gadget online'); one to 'Live More' (for example, 'Have a swapshop party – get your friends together to swap DVDs, books or clothes you don't want anymore'). A special Lent 'credit card' was produced to remind people to 'think before they spend'.

FOR YOUR FOLDER

1. What is the purpose of Lent?
2. Do you think Lent has any value for Christians today? Give reasons for your answer.
3. Explain the role of fasting, prayer and almsgiving (charity) in the season of Lent.
4. Why do Catholics receive ashes on Ash Wednesday?

IN A GROUP

1. Discuss the view that it is more valuable for Christians to take up good habits during Lent than to give things up.
2. Advent is a more important time than Lent. Do you agree or disagree? Give reasons for your answer.

HOLY WEEK AND EASTER SUNDAY

Holy Week is the last week of Lent ending with Easter Sunday. During this week Christians remember the last events in the life of Christ, particularly his suffering and death. Each of the events in the last week of Jesus' life is remembered at some point during Holy Week.

Palm Sunday

The Sunday before Easter Sunday remembers the triumphal entry of Jesus into Jerusalem on a donkey. The people waved palm branches in honour of him and shouted 'hosanna'. Today **palm crosses** are given out in some churches.

Holy Thursday or Maundy Thursday

This remembers the events of the Last Supper Jesus had with his disciples before his death.

The word *maundy* means 'commandment'. At the last supper Jesus gave his disciples a new commandment "*to love one another*" (John 15:12), and gave a practical demonstration by taking the role of a servant, washing his disciple's feet. Every year the Pope carries out foot washing at a special service.

In England, the monarch used to wash the feet of the poor, but this has now been replaced by the giving of 'maundy money' to the elderly.

In the Catholic Church special services are held to bless the **anointing oils** that will be used for sacraments throughout the year.

After the Last Supper, Jesus prayed in the Garden of Gethsemane before he was arrested. Some churches hold all night prayer vigils in memory of this night.

Good Friday

Good Friday remembers the day that Jesus died. It is a day of sadness and somber reflection on the death of Jesus. It is called 'Good' because of the Christian understanding of Jesus' death – a willing sacrifice that redeems the world to God. People have the chance to have their sins forgiven and to enter into the Kingdom of God.

Special services and prayer vigils are held. Many use the symbol of a candle being blown out to recall Jesus' death. Some Christians fast on Good Friday as a sign of sorrow.

Holy Saturday

Jesus' body was taken down from the cross and buried in a tomb provided by Joseph of Arimathea. The Catholic Church holds an Easter vigil to prepare for the day ahead.

Easter Sunday

Easter Sunday is the central festival of the Church year. It recalls Jesus' Resurrection from the dead. Easter vigils that begin on Holy Saturday light Easter fires or 'Paschal candles' at midnight. Dawn services are held at a variety of outdoor venues including seaside and hill top locations where people sing worship songs and watch the sun rise – an appropriate symbol of Christ's Resurrection.

Regular Sunday services take on an air of celebration. Buildings are decorated with flowers, music may feature various instruments, and church bells are rung. Easter Sunday is also a traditional day for new Christians who have been undergoing training and instruction to be baptised.

FOR YOUR FOLDER

Copy the table below and use the accounts of people's Easter experiences to complete it.

Teresa:
"I attend the Catholic Church and we have a number of ceremonies to celebrate Holy Week. Good Friday is a very solemn day and we don't celebrate Mass. All the statues in the church are covered. It is a day of mourning. We have a service at 3 pm where we remember the Passion of Jesus by praying the Stations of the Cross. In the evening there is another solemn service. We all process to the altar and kiss the Cross. The Easter vigil on Saturday night is an amazing experience. The Mass really emphasises the theme of light overcoming darkness and we all light candles from one another in the darkness of the Church."

Graham:
"In St Anne's Church of Ireland Cathedral there is a special service on Good Friday called the 'Service of the Three Hours'. It lasts from 12 pm until 3pm and is made up of a series of 25 minute services of music, prayer, praise and readings, which highlight aspects of the crucifixion. People are free to come and go, which suits those who can only get a short break from work. It is a great chance for me to take time out of the rush of the day and to think about what Christ has done for me."

David:
"I am part of a Methodist Church and on Easter Sunday every year I get up early to celebrate Christ's Resurrection at a dawn service. Sometimes an Easter fire is lit to keep everyone warm. We sing and pray together and read the Gospel accounts of the Resurrection. Often, we share communion together."

Tony:
"Easter is a very important time for my Baptist Church. We have communion on Palm Sunday in the evening, and on Maundy Thursday we have a joint service with a neighbouring Baptist Church. On Easter Sunday there is a big celebration service to remember the Resurrection. Then on Easter Monday we meet in the afternoon in the Church grounds for a treasure hunt, which is followed by a barbecue."

Laura:
"On Good Friday my church meet with other congregations in the local area. Presbyterians, Methodists, Catholics, all praying and worshipping together. Events like these really bring people together and show the friendship and unity we share as followers of Jesus."

Holy Week in the Christian Church		
Day	**Why is it remembered?**	**How is it remembered?**
Palm Sunday		
Holy Thursday or Maundy Thursday		
Good Friday		
Holy Saturday		
Easter Sunday		

CHRISTIANITY

IN A GROUP

Read the following articles and discuss the questions below:

RELIGIOUS HOLIDAY TO BE AXED

By KAMEL ADMED, Political Editor

Schools are to be told to scrap Easter holidays and replace them with a non-religious 'spring break' as part of a fundamental overhaul of the way children are taught.

Despite objections from the Church of England and Christian pressure groups, supporters of the proposals say a specific Easter holiday is incompatible with a modern school system because it is on a different date each year. Moving to a fixed holiday would reduce teacher stress and pupil truancy and improve exam results.

The proposals say schools should be more ready to celebrate non-Christian festivals such as Diwali and the end of Ramadan. Head teachers will be allowed 10 'flexible days' each year to hold holidays which reflect the ethnic make-up of the school."

Source: *The Observer*, 27 May 2001. http://www.guardian.co.uk/ uk/2001/may/27/schools

TRADITIONAL EASTER SCHOOL BREAK TO BE AXED

Hundreds of Mersey schools will ... scrap the traditional Easter break. It is an attempt to make life easier for families who live, work and go to school across council boundaries. The five participating authorities confirmed they will press ahead with the overhaul after winning support from the majority of parents, teachers and church officials.

Currently, term times can vary, making it difficult for teachers and parents to plan ahead because the two-week Easter holiday coincides with religious celebrations. Easter Sunday can fall anywhere between March 22 and April 25. But, under the unified model, Easter holidays will be replaced by a set 'spring break' during the first two weeks of April.

If Easter falls outside that time, schools will not open on Good Friday or Easter Monday. Schools will break up for summer towards the end of July until the end of August. The changes will be reviewed in 2011 to see how well they are working.

In Liverpool, 82% of people backed the alterations.

Taken from an original article by Ben Turner, *Liverpool Daily Post*, 30 July 2009, http://www.liverpooldailypost.co.uk/liverpool-news/ regional-news/2009/07/30/merseyside-schools-to-synchronise-term- times-92534-24273128/

1. Do you think churches can learn from each other's traditions regarding the celebration of festivals? Give reasons for your answer.

2. Do you think Easter should still be celebrated as a religious holiday in the twenty-first century? Explain your answer.

3. If Easter holidays in schools were replaced by a spring break, do you think it would make Easter seem less important? Make a list of arguments for and against this proposal.

SYMBOLS ASSOCIATED WITH EASTER

The Cross

Why would someone wear a symbol of execution around their neck?

The cross did not appear as a symbol for Christianity until the second century because it was seen as offensive. It was the worst form of torture and death imaginable, reserved for the lowest criminals and traitors. Roman citizens would not even mention crucifixion.

For centuries the cross has been worn as a simple expression of Christian faith. In the last hundred years it has become a popular item of jewellery and this has lead to some controversial discussion.

Some people object to the cross being worn as a fashion accessory: The death of Jesus is to be remembered with reverence, and the fact that the cross is sold as a trendy pendant in High Street stores is outrageous.

Other Christians argue that the Jesus is central to our culture, and the development of the cross into a fashion item shows that there is a deep, spiritual longing to connect with something meaningful. In a world of worries, change and fractured lives, the cross points to something deep and unchanging.

IN A GROUP

"A cross or crucifix should only be worn by people who appreciate its true meaning". Do you agree or disagree? Discuss your reasons.

Light

Light is a very important symbol for Christians. Jesus said *"I am the Light of the World"* (John 8:12), and taught his followers to shine like lights (Matthew 5:14). Some Good Friday services end with the blowing out of a single candle – a powerful symbol of Christ's death.

In the Catholic Easter Vigil Mass there is a solemn procession through a darkened Church carrying the **Paschal** candle. Each member of the congregation lights a smaller candle from the Paschal Candle or from each other, symbolising the light of Christ being passed on. The light symbolises:

- **Life** – Jesus' Resurrection brings new Life because he overcame death which is symbolised by darkness.
- **Knowledge** – Lack of knowledge is sometimes described as darkness of mind. The mind which is full of knowledge and wisdom is said to be 'enlightened'.

New Life

These symbols all have pre-Christian roots. Spring was celebrated as the coming forth of new life. The Easter Egg is the most well-known symbol associated with Easter. This became an appropriate symbol for the Christian celebration – new life breaking out of the tomb.

FOR YOUR FOLDER

1. What event is remembered on Good Friday?
2. Do you think that Easter should have a fixed annual date just like Christmas? Explain your answer.
3. Describe how Easter is celebrated in the Christian Church.
4. "Christmas is a more important festival than Easter." Do you agree or disagree?

PENTECOST

Pentecost is a celebration of the coming of the Holy Spirit which was promised by Jesus (John 14:16). The Holy Spirit gave the followers of Jesus power to go out and spread the Gospel, as Jesus had commanded them to do. Over three thousand people were converted to Christianity on the Day of Pentecost, so it is sometimes celebrated as the 'birthday' of the Church. Pentecost falls fifty days after Easter.

In some churches Pentecost is called 'Whitsun'. It was a tradition that baptisms would be carried out at this time of year, which meant the church would be full of newly baptised people wearing white robes. It became known as 'White Sunday', and then 'Whitsun'.

In some churches the Day of Pentecost is also a time to thank God for the gifts of the Holy Spirit. Symbolism such as flames of fire or a white dove could be displayed on church walls at Pentecost. These symbols remind believers about the power of God and the peace that the Holy Spirit brings.

FOR YOUR FOLDER

1. Explain why Pentecost is important to Christians.
2. "Pentecost is as important for Christians as Christmas or Easter. It should be a public holiday." Do you agree or disagree? Give reasons, showing that you have considered more than one point of view.

SAINT'S DAYS

Saints days are celebrated in the Church of Ireland and the Catholic Church. In the early Church the term 'saint' referred to follower of Jesus. As the church grew and developed, 'saint' came to mean those who lived a life of exemplary holiness and devotion to God. They showed they were close to God by the choices they made and the way they lived their life. Some served others in a selfless way; others brought people to the faith by their preaching, teaching and example. Some were even prepared to die for their faith. They are called **Martyrs.**

FURTHER THINKING

Saint Stephen was the first Christian martyr. What can you find out about Saint Stephen's day?

All Saint's Day

This celebration on 1 November was originally instituted to honour all the Christian martyrs, but has extended to remembering all the Christian saints. It is a holy day of Obligation in the Catholic Church, which means Catholics should mark the day by attending Mass.

Patron Saints

It became common practice in the Catholic Church to seek the prayers of saints for certain things. Gradually, certain saints came to be seen as guardians of a place, trade or group. Often, this would relate to the things the saint was interested in during their lifetime. For example, Saint Joseph became the patron saint of carpenters. Some saints who suffered particular illnesses, or cared for those who did, became patron saints for that disease or illness.

St Francis of Assisi

St Francis of Assisi is the patron saint of animals. It is customary for Anglican and Roman Catholic churches to hold ceremonies blessing animals on his feast day of 4 October.

FOR YOUR FOLDER

1. What is a saint?
2. Explain the role of saints in the Catholic Church.
3. What is a Patron saint?

 HARVEST

The Harvest festival is mainly celebrated in Protestant churches. It is a time to thank God for the food we eat, and for all that God provides. Harvest Thanksgiving Services take place in the autumn and, in the past, would have been associated with farmers bringing in their crops to supply the local community with enough food to last the year.

Church buildings are decorated with flowers, fruit and vegetables. There may be a table for people to bring gifts of food, which will later be distributed to the poor, or elderly people stuck at home. Bible readings and hymns will be carefully chosen to reflect the theme of God's provision. The service is also a chance for Christians to be reminded of those who do not have enough food. During the service there will be prayers for countries suffering from starvation and the congregation may make a donation to a charity helping people suffering in the developing world.

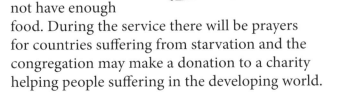

Why celebrate saints' days?

- Some Christians believe that it is important to celebrate saints' days to **remember** the great men and women of the Church. They have done great things for the Church and their achievements are celebrated with a special day in their honour.

- Saints are also an **inspiration** to other Christians. They are good examples of commitment to the faith and love and service of God and neighbour.

- The Catholic Church believes that saints are already in heaven and are especially close to God. This means that Christians can ask the saint to pray on their behalf. This is viewed similarly to asking a friend to pray for you.

The Container Ministry

FOR YOUR FOLDER

1. Explain what different churches do to thank God for the harvest.
2. Do you think harvest thanksgiving services have any relevance today?

IN A GROUP

"The Church today spends too much time focusing on past events and not enough on meeting the needs of people living in the twenty-first century."

Do you agree or disagree? Give reasons for your answer showing you have considered different points of view.

One example of an organisation working to provide appropriate resources to developing countries is the Container Ministry. Based in Lurgan, Co Armagh, the Container Ministry is part of the Methodist Missionary Society (Ireland).

People donate items such as computers, tools, educational resources and hospital equipment which volunteers assess and load into container lorries which are shipped across the world. This is in response to specific requests from overseas partner churches.

A Prayer for the Container Ministry

Thank you, God, that we live in a prosperous land with a temperate climate.

Forgive us when we take for granted your blessings, waste your gifts, dump good food, and are poor stewards of valuable resources.

Thank you for the work of the Container Ministry … We ask for your continued provision for the Container ministry to re-cycle and provide new products in the service of the world Church.

Give safe passage by land and sea and through customs at point of entry.

Guide this ministry as it changes to meet the changing needs of the world.

We offer this prayer in the name of our Lord Jesus Christ who fed the hungry, blessed the children, healed the sick and preached the good news to the poor.

Amen

Source: http://www.irishmethodist.org/mmsi/container.htm

Chapter 6

SACRAMENTS AND ORDINANCES

A sacrament is a formal religious ceremony which St Augustine described as "A visible sign of an invisible reality". Taking part in ceremonies like Baptism or Communion enables people to focus on God and experience God in a particular way. The Presbyterian, Methodist, Church of Ireland and Catholic churches all accept that God's grace is given in a special way to a person when they receive a sacrament.

The Baptist Church does not believe that any special grace is given through these ceremonies. They are seen as simply symbolic. The Baptist Church does not use the word 'sacrament', but refers to Baptism and Communion as **ordinances** because they were instituted and ordained by Jesus.

Most Protestant denominations recognise baptism and communion as sacraments or ordinances. The Quakers and the Salvation Army have no sacraments or ordinances. The Catholic Church recognises seven sacraments: Baptism; Confirmation; Eucharist; Reconciliation (confession); Anointing of the sick; Marriage and Holy Orders (becoming a Priest).

This chapter will look at Catholic and Protestant approaches to Baptism and Eucharist (Communion).

Churches differ on whether people should be baptised as infants or as adults, and on what exactly the symbolism of Baptism means.

TEACHER'S NOTE

For this section, those studying module 3.1 'The Christian Church through a study of the Catholic Church and One Protestant Tradition' should study the material on the Catholic Church and select one Protestant denomination.

Those studying module 3.2a 'The Christian Church with a focus on the Catholic Church' should study the material on the Catholic Church only.

Those studying module 3.2b 'The Christian Church with a focus on the Protestant Tradition' should study material on two Protestant denominations.
(Continue reading from page 99.)

 **BAPTISM**

Baptism is a symbolic washing in water that is often seen as a ceremony of initiation into the Church. Jesus himself was baptised and in the Great Commission orders his followers:
"Go, then, to all peoples everywhere and make them my disciples: baptise them in the name of the Father, the Son, and the Holy Spirit" (Matthew 28:19).

BAPTISM IN THE CATHOLIC CHURCH

There are three main points about baptism in the Catholic Church. These will be considered in more detail in the following section:

1. Baptism is a sacrament.
2. It is for the infants of members of the Catholic Church, or adults who have not been baptised.
3. It is carried out by pouring water over the head three times.

WHO IS BAPTISED?

The Catholic Church baptises infants as a sign of becoming part of God's family, the Church. This usually happens in the first few weeks of the child's life. Sometimes adults who have not already been baptised can receive the sacrament.

THE ROLE OF GODPARENTS

In the Catholic Church, people, usually family friends, are chosen to be godparents. They are representative of the Christian family and agree to support the parents in bringing the child up in the faith. During the ceremony the priest will ask the godparents whether they are prepared to help the parents in this way. For this reason the Catholic Church asks that one of the godparents is a Catholic themselves.

CEREMONY OF BAPTISM IN THE CATHOLIC CHURCH

Baptisms usually take place every week. There may be just one family presenting a child, or a few baptisms at the same time. The Easter service will sometimes include baptism. People invite family and friends to join them at the ceremony.

The baptism ceremony can be divided into four parts:

1. At the Door

The ceremony of baptism begins at the door of the Church. This is symbolic of the child's entrance into the Christian Community. Here the priest will ask the name which is to be given to the infant and outline the responsibility of the parents and the godparents. He will say:

> "You have asked to have your child baptised. In doing so you are accepting the responsibility of training him in the practice of the faith. It will be your duty to bring him up according to God's Commandments as Christ taught us by loving God and our neighbour …"

The priest will then ask the godparents if they are willing to help the parents in this task. Then the child is welcomed into the Christian family with the words,

> "(Name), the Christian community welcomes you with great joy. In its name I claim you for Christ our Saviour by the sign of his cross. I now trace the sign of the Cross on your forehead and invite your parents and godparents to do the same."

2. At the Book

The next stage of the ceremony takes place at the Book. Scripture readings usually include the story of the baptism of Jesus or his conversation with Nicodemus (John 3:1–21). There will be a short explanation of the readings after which there will be **'Prayers of the Faithful'** for the child, parents and godparents. The child is then anointed on the chest with the **Oil of Catechumens** sometimes called the **Oil of Salvation.**

> "We anoint you with the oil of Salvation in the name of Christ our Saviour: may he strengthen you with his power …"

3. At the Font

The priest blesses the water with which the baby will be baptised. The parents and the godparents are asked to renew their own faith promises – another reminder of their responsibility to bring the child up in the faith.

> "Dear parents and Godparents … On your part you must make it your constant care to bring him/her up in the practise of the faith …"

The baptismal promises are made on behalf of the child in the form of question and answer:

> "Do you reject Satan and all his works and all his empty promises?
>
> "Do you believe in God the Father Almighty, creator of heaven and earth?
>
> "Do you believe in Jesus Christ, his only son our Lord, who was born of the Virgin Mary, was crucified, died and was buried, rose from the dead and is now seated at the right hand of the Father?"

The parents reply "We Do."

The water is poured three times over the forehead of the baby with the words:

> "(Name), I baptise you in the name of the Father and of the Son and of the Holy Spirit"

The child is then anointed with the **Oil of Chrism**. The baptismal candle is lit by one of the parents from the paschal candle (which represents Jesus' Resurrection). The priest says:

> "Receive the light of Christ … to be kept burning brightly … this child of yours is to walk always as a child of the light. May he/she keep the flame of faith alive in his/her heart."

4. At the Altar

The child and their family look forward to the Eucharist, the second **sacrament of Initiation** into the Church. Everyone says the **'Our Father'** and prayers are offered for the mother and father and for all those who have attended the baptism.

The priest touches the baby's ears and mouth and prays that they may receive God's word and proclaim the faith.

BELIEFS ABOUT BAPTISM

Baptism is one of the seven sacraments of the Catholic Church. It is the first of the sacraments of initiation which will make the person a full member of the Church.

These sacraments of initiation are **Baptism, Eucharist and Confirmation.** Baptism is usually administered by a priest but any Catholic can carry out baptism. This may be necessary in an emergency, if someone becomes ill.

Catholics believe that:

- In the sacrament of Baptism the child first meets the risen Jesus
- The child begins a new life in Christ
- The child receives the grace of God
- The child becomes a member of the Church
- The child is cleansed of Original sin
- The child first receives the Holy Spirit but will receive the fullness of the Spirit at Confirmation

> The Sacraments of initiation, Baptism, Confirmation and the Eucharist lay the foundations of every Christian life ... The faithful are born anew by baptism, strengthened by the sacrament of Confirmation, and receive in the Eucharist the food of eternal life.
>
> *Catechism of the Catholic Church (1212)*

SYMBOLISM OF BAPTISM

1. Water

Water is the central symbol of baptism. The Catholic Church teaches that human beings are born sinful (original sin), so Baptism is seen as washing away the stain of sin.

Water is also a powerful symbol in the Old Testament:

- In the Creation story in Genesis 1:1–10 it is a source of **power** and **strength.**
- In the story of Noah, God sent the flood in punishment for man's sins, so it can be a symbol of **death.**
- In Exodus 14:15–31 it sets people **free** from slavery and so is a sign of **hope** and **new beginnings.**

In Catholic Baptism, water signifies **death to the old, sinful self**, **freedom from the power of evil** and **new life in Christ**.

2. Anointing Oils

The **oil of salvation** symbolises that the child is given the strength to fight against evil and to do good. The oil of **chrism** is used to show that the child has now been given the task **of carrying out the work of Christ**, just as people in the Old Testament were anointed for special tasks.

3. Paschal Candle

The Paschal Candle represents Christ overcoming death and sin in the same way as light overcomes darkness.

4. White Garment

In Catholic baptism the baby is always clothed in a white garment. In baptism they have *"become clothed in Christ"* (Galatians 3:27). It is a sign of happiness, new life, innocence and sinlessness.

5. Name

The chosen name of the child is sometimes a saint's name. The child can try to live up to the qualities of that saint.

6. The sign of the Cross

The sign of the cross traced on the child's forehead is a symbol of ownership – the child now belongs to God the Father.

Claire

" Before Sean was even born, my husband and I began to discuss his baptism. For us, it was a very important family and religious occasion. We had thought about asking a priest who had celebrated our marriage to baptise him, but then realised it was important for Sean to begin his journey into the Christian faith by being baptised by the local priest who would be there for Sean's First Holy Communion. We used the christening robe my sister used to baptise her children, and chose an uncle and aunt to be the godparents – people who would always be there for Sean to guide him in his faith. Baptism for us is the first step for Sean in his Christian faith. "

BAPTISM IN THE CHURCH OF IRELAND

There are three main points about baptism in the Church of Ireland. These will be considered in more detail in the following section:

1. Baptism is a sacrament.
2. It is for the infants of believers or for adults who were not baptised as infants.
3. It is carried out by pouring water three times over the person's head.

WHO IS BAPTISED?

The Church of Ireland usually baptises infants, normally in the first few weeks of the child's life as a sign of acceptance into the family of the Church. Sometimes adults who have not already been baptised can receive the sacrament.

THE ROLE OF GODPARENTS

Usually, family friends are chosen to be godparents, also known as sponsors. During the ceremony they promise to support the parents in bringing the child up in the faith. It is considered a privilege and a responsibility.

A CEREMONY OF BAPTISM IN THE CHURCH OF IRELAND

Most baptisms are carried out in public in front of the local congregation as the ceremony is a sign of welcoming the child into the family of the church. The sacrament of baptism takes place after the ministry of the word.

At the baptism the parents and godparents are required to make promises on behalf of the child and to undertake to "encourage them in the life and faith of the Christian Community" and to "care for them, and help them to take their place within the life and worship of Christ's Church" (*Book of Common Prayer*, page 361).

The parents and the godparents are asked three questions:

- Do you turn to Christ?
- Do you renounce the Devil and all his works?
- Will you obey and serve Christ?

The water is blessed at the font. The parents are asked to affirm the Apostles' Creed. The minister then holds the infant, pours water over its head three times, while saying the words:

> *"(Name), I baptise you in the Name of the Father and of the Son and of the Holy Spirit."*

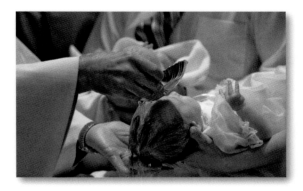

The minister makes the sign of the cross on the infant's forehead.

As baptism is the beginning of the Christian life, a lighted candle may be presented with the words "You have received the light of Christ; walk in this light all the days of your life. Shine as a light in the world to the glory of God the Father" (*Book of Common Prayer*, page 367).

The congregation welcomes the infant into the church with the words:

> *"God has adopted you by baptism into his church. We therefore receive you into the household of faith, as a member of the body of Christ, as the child of the same heavenly Father, and as an inheritor with us of the kingdom of God."*

Everyone recites the Lord's Prayer.

After the infant is baptised a baptismal card is issued. This is an official record that the baptism has taken place.

BELIEFS ABOUT BAPTISM

The Church of Ireland describes baptism as:

> "union with Christ in his death and Resurrection, the forgiveness of sins, and a new birth into God's family."
>
> *The Revised Catechism*

At baptism, a person receives forgiveness and a new life in Christ and becomes part of Christ's body, the Church. This begins the journey of the Christian life. When the child is old enough to understand they can take their own vows at a service of confirmation.

SYMBOLISM OF BAPTISM

1. Water

Water symbolises cleansing from sin and the beginning of New Life.

2. The Sign of the Cross

The minister makes the sign of the cross on the infant's forehead during the baptism, as a visible sign of belonging to Christ: "Christ claims you for his own. Receive the sign of the cross. Live as a disciple of Christ" (*Book of Common Prayer*, page 362).

3. White Garment

In the Church of Ireland, the baby is usually clothed in a white garment. In baptism they have *"become clothed in Christ"* (Galatians 3:27). It is a sign of happiness, new life, innocence and sinlessness.

BAPTISM IN THE BAPTIST CHURCH

There are three main points to remember about baptism in the Baptist Church. These will be considered in more detail in the following section:

1. Baptism is considered to be an ordinance, not a sacrament.
2. It is for believing Christians only.
3. It is by total immersion in water.

WHO IS BAPTISED?

Baptist Churches do not baptise infants. They argue that a person wanting to be baptised should be a professing Christian, and should be old enough to understand why there is a need for baptism. The type of baptism carried out in the Baptist church is called 'believers' baptism'. The youngest people who are baptised in the Baptist Church have usually reached secondary school age.

A CEREMONY OF BAPTISM IN THE BAPTIST CHURCH

In the Baptist church baptism always takes place in public because it is a public confession of faith in Christ. Those to be baptised invite friends and family. The ceremony usually happens at the end of a Sunday worship service. The ceremony includes the following parts:

The baptismal tank is opened and the pastor, dressed in casual clothes, will get into the tank, which is filled waist deep in water.

The person being baptised will follow the pastor into the tank. Normally, men wear a white shirt and trousers and women wear a special robe.

The Pastor will ask the candidate for baptism:

"*Do you now confess Jesus Christ as your Lord and Saviour?*"

The candidate answers:

"*I do*"

The candidate may now take the opportunity to tell those gathered about how they became a Christian and why they want to be baptised.

The candidate for baptism clasps their hands in front of their chest. The pastor puts one of his hands on the person's hands and the other one behind the person's back. The pastor then says:

"*On profession of your faith in the Lord Jesus Christ as your personal Saviour, I now baptise you in the name of the Father and of the Son and of the Holy Spirit. Amen.*"

The pastor then plunges the person under the water until they are completely immersed, and immediately pulls the person out of the water again.

The newly baptised person then climbs up the steps and leaves the tank to go and get changed. The congregation sings a hymn. The baptism is followed by a celebration of the Lord's Supper.

The candidate receives a Certificate of Baptism which gives details of the name of the person baptised, the date, the pastor's name and the name of the local church.

BELIEFS ABOUT BAPTISM

Baptists do not believe that there is any special power or presence of God during the ceremony of Baptism. It is simply symbolic. Baptism was instituted and ordained by Jesus for the church, to strengthen believers. For this reason, Baptists refer to baptism as an **ordinance**, not a **sacrament**.

After baptism the person becomes a full member of the church. It is a serious commitment, and a way of formalising a person's faith. Baptism is considered 'outward expression of an inward change', and a clear commitment to turn from sinful ways.

SYMBOLISM OF BAPTISM

Baptists believe that baptism should be by **total immersion**:

"Immersion, or dipping of the person in water, is necessary to the due administration of this ordinance."

Things Most Surely Believed among Us,
The Baptist Confession of Faith, with Scripture Proofs, of 1689

In the Baptist tradition, the symbolism of baptism reflects Paul's teaching in Romans 6:3–5:

"For surely you know that when we were baptised into union with Christ Jesus, we were baptised into union with his death. By our baptism, then, we were buried with him and shared his death, in order that, just as Christ was raised from death by the glorious power of the Father, so also we might live a new life. For since we have become one with him in dying as he did, in the same way we shall be one with him by being raised to life as he was."

- Being immersed under the water = dying to old, sinful way of life
- Being under the water = being buried with Christ
- Coming out of the water = rising to a new life in Christ

BAPTISM IN THE METHODIST CHURCH

There are three main points about baptism in the Methodist Church. These will be considered in more detail in the following section:

1. Baptism is a sacrament.
2. It is for the infants of believers or for children and adults who were not baptised as infants.
3. It is carried out by pouring or sprinkling water over the person's head.

Baptism by immersion is a symbol of sharing in the death, burial and Resurrection of Christ.

The physical falling back into the water is a symbolic burial. This is a sign of change and repentance (turning from your sins). The change is so drastic that the old person is 'buried'.

The rising up out of the water is a symbol of resurrection. The old, sinful self is buried, and the new self is alive.

The message of life change is clear. It is as if the person is saying: "my old life is behind me – I am a new person, with a new life."

IS BAPTISM NECESSARY FOR NEW MEMBERS OF THE BAPTIST CHURCH?

Some people who were baptised as children might move churches and want to join a local Baptist congregation. Normally, Baptist churches do not require them to be rebaptised, as long as they have made another adult declaration of faith, such as confirmation in the Church of Ireland.

WHO IS BAPTISED?

The children of Christian parents are usually baptised as infants in the Methodist Church. The *Methodist Service Book* also explains that older children and adults can also receive the sacrament of baptism.

THE ROLE OF SPONSORS

In the Methodist Church parents can bring relatives and family friends to act as sponsors. The church also provides a sponsor, usually someone involved in children's ministry. During the ceremony they promise to support the parents in bringing the child up in the faith. It is considered a privilege and a responsibility.

A CEREMONY OF BAPTISM IN THE METHODIST CHURCH

Baptisms take place in public, usually during the Sunday morning worship service. This is because at baptism a child is welcomed into the fellowship of the church. The order of the baptismal service is set out in the *Methodist Service Book*.

The parents and sponsors bring the child to the font, where the Bible is read.

The congregation promise to:

> "maintain the common life of worship and service that he/she and all children among you may grow in grace and in the knowledge and love of God and of his Son Jesus Christ."

The parents promise to bring the child up in the way of Christ by teaching and guiding the child in Christian ways.

The minister asks the child's name and makes the sign of the cross on its forehead using water from the font:

> "(Name), I baptise you in the Name of the Father, and of the Son and of the Holy Spirit."

The child may be presented with a Bible as a reminder of the baptism.

In some cases a lit candle may be presented by the church sponsor with the words:

> "I give you this sign, for you now belong to Christ, the light of the world."

The minister will then pray for the child and their family.

BELIEFS ABOUT BAPTISM

In the Methodist Church baptism is a sign and seal that a person has become a member of God's family, the Church.

The child is too young to even realise the power of God's love, and it is hoped that when the child is

older they will make a personal profession of faith and agree to live by their baptismal vows. Methodists believe that it is possible to be a Christian without being baptised.

SYMBOLISM OF BAPTISM

1. Water

Water symbolises cleansing from sin and the beginning of New Life.

2. The Sign of the Cross

The minister makes the sign of the cross on the infant's forehead during the baptism, as a sign that they belong to Christ.

3. Candle

This is a symbol that the child belongs to Christ, the Light of the World, and is invited to 'shine', as Jesus directed in Matthew 5:16.

BAPTISM IN THE PRESBYTERIAN CHURCH

There are three main points about baptism in the Presbyterian Church. These will be considered in more detail in the following section:

1. Baptism is a sacrament.
2. It is for the infants of believers or for adults who were not baptised as infants.
3. It is usually carried out by sprinkling water over the person's head.

WHO IS BAPTISED?

Presbyterians baptise infants, although people can be baptised as adults. A minister can refuse to baptise if he feels the parents do not meet certain criteria – they must be practicing Christians and regular church attenders.

A CEREMONY OF BAPTISM IN THE PRESBYTERIAN CHURCH

Baptism takes place in public in front of the local congregation. It usually forms part of a normal Sunday morning service.

The parents and minister stand at the font. The minister asks the parents two questions:

> *"In presenting this child for baptism do you profess your faith in God as your Creator and Father, in Jesus Christ as your Lord and Saviour, and in the Holy Spirit as you Sanctifier and Guide?"*

> *"Will you, by God's help, provide a Christian home and bring up this child in the worship and teaching of the church, so that your child may come to know Jesus Christ as Lord and Saviour?"*

The parents answer, "We do".

The minister holds the child and makes the sign of the cross on its forehead using water from the font:

> *"In the name of the Father, the Son and the Holy Spirit, I baptise you (name of child)."*

> *"We now receive this child into the fellowship of the Church and promise to order our congregational life that he/she may grow up in the knowledge and love of God."*

The congregation then sings the Aaronic Blessing to welcome the child into the fellowship of the church:

> *"The Lord bless you and keep you. The Lord make his face to shine upon you and be gracious onto you. The Lord lift up his countenance upon you and give you peace."*

BELIEFS ABOUT BAPTISM

Presbyterians do not believe that baptism makes a child a Christian. Rather, it is a sign to show the work of the grace of God. Presbyterians believe that what matters most in baptism is what God is doing for his people – and not what they do. Infant baptism looks forward to a time when the child will have his or her own personal faith.

Presbyterians understand baptism as an outward sign of entering into a **Covenant** with God. In the Old Testament the Covenant with God was sealed with the physical sign of circumcision (Genesis 17:10). The Covenant changed with Christ, and so did the symbol – from circumcision to baptism.

Just as whole households were circumcised to mark themselves out as being in Covenant with God, so Presbyterians baptise whole households to mark them out as being in Covenant with God through Jesus.

Through baptism the child becomes a member of the Church, the body of Christ.

SYMBOLISM OF BAPTISM

Water

Baptism is carried out by pouring or sprinkling water on the person. This was the main way that ceremonial purification was carried out in the Old Testament.

Presbyterians believe that just as water makes people clean, so baptism pictures how God, through Jesus Christ, can make a person's whole life clean, forgiving their sins and giving new life in the Holy Spirit.

Blessing

The Aaronic Blessing is a priestly blessing from the Old Testament (Numbers 6:24–26). The congregation sing it as a way of welcoming the new child into the congregation.

BELIEVERS' BAPTISM VERSUS INFANT BAPTISM

The debate about how baptism should be performed has been going on for centuries. Most Christian churches baptise both infants and adults, but some believe that baptism should only be for adults.

The Catholic Church, Church of Ireland, Presbyterian Church and Methodist Church all practice baptism for both infants and adults. They recognise baptism performed in any of these denominations as valid, subject to certain conditions. It is only possible to be baptised once, so people who change denomination are not baptised again.

ARGUMENTS FOR BELIEVER'S BAPTISM

The Baptist Church, and some other groups, do not accept infant baptism at all. They have three main arguments:

1. Believer's baptism is the only kind of baptism seen in the New Testament.

2. Baptism cannot make someone a Christian. It is an outward sign of inward change.

3. Infants are not old enough to understand what they are doing. Baptism is only meaningful if it is a personal choice.

In the New Testament, baptism is a sign that someone has been changed and wants to follow Christ. Baptism is for those who have turned away from their sin and put their faith in the Lord Jesus Christ, and who are committed to living his way.

People should be baptised because it is the command of Christ:

> "*Go and make disciples of all nations, baptising them in the name of the Father, the Son and the Holy Spirit*" (Matthew 28.19).

From the very beginning, the Church has baptised those who want to follow Jesus (Acts 2:38–41).

Baptism should be by full immersion in water. This was the practice in the New Testament and it best symbolises the death, burial and Resurrection of Jesus with which Christians are identifying. Examples can be found in Matthew 3:16, Acts 8:38 and Romans 6:1–4. The Greek word *baptizo* used in these texts means 'to dip' or to 'submerge'.

Although churches that support infant baptism would say otherwise, there is no conclusive evidence of infant baptism occurring in the Bible.

ARGUMENTS FOR INFANT BAPTISM

Infant baptism is practiced in the Church of Ireland and the Presbyterian, Methodist and Catholic churches. Each has a slightly different understanding of baptism, but all agree that baptism is the ceremony which brings new babies into the community of faith. The main arguments for infant baptism are explained below:

1. Baptism is a sign of becoming part of the Christian community and beginning a spiritual journey, so it is appropriate that people are baptised as children.

2. Some Christians believe that baptism is a sacrament in which people experience God's grace. Children should not be excluded from these experiences.

3. There is evidence of infant baptism in the Bible.

For Presbyterians especially, the Old Testament symbolism of Covenant is an important part of baptism. From Genesis 17:10 onwards the people used circumcision to mark themselves out as God's people. Jewish boys are circumcised when they are eight days old as a sign of the Covenant with God. Likewise, the children of Christian parents are baptised as a sign of being God's people under the **New Covenant** (see page 107).

In Genesis 17:9–14 it was commanded that every male in the **whole household** should be circumcised. Likewise, there is evidence of 'Household Baptism' in the New Testament, notably in Acts 16:15 and Acts 16:31–33. Churches that teach adult baptism only would argue that these verses are inconclusive.

THE CATHOLIC VIEW

For Catholics, baptism is the beginning of the faith journey. Through baptism, children become members of God's family, the Church; are cleansed from original sin; and receive God's grace and the Holy Spirit.

Throughout their lives, the baptised person will continue to grow and receive God's grace through other sacraments at key times in the their life. For example, the sacrament of Confirmation as they begin the journey into adulthood; the sacrament of Marriage or Holy Orders; the sacrament of Anointing the Sick when they are ill.

It is argued that the child will benefit from being brought up in the faith of their parents and from belonging to a believing community.

While an infant is unable to make baptismal promises for themselves, everyone has the chance to renew the promises every year, during the Sacrament of Confirmation at the Easter Vigil.

CLASS DEBATE

Look at the cases for infant baptism and believers' baptism.

Summarise the main points of each argument, including Bible references.

Organise a class debate on which form of baptism is more acceptable.

IN A GROUP

Some of the reasons Christians give for baptism are influenced by the preference for either infant or believers' baptism.

Look at each of the following reasons in turn and discuss whether each supports infant baptism, believers' baptism or both:

Reasons for Baptism

- It grants salvation
- It takes away sin
- It commemorates Christ's death and Resurrection
- It fulfils Jesus' command to baptise
- It confers God's grace
- It is a public expression of faith

FOR YOUR FOLDER

1. Explain the difference between infant baptism and believer's baptism.

2. "It is the responsibility of all Christian parents to make sure that their children are baptised as babies."
   Do you agree or disagree? Give reasons for your answer showing that you have considered different points of view.

3. Do you think that the promises made in baptism should be publicly renewed on a regular basis? Give reasons for your answer.

EUCHARIST OR COMMUNION

Eucharist or Communion refers to a symbolic meal of bread and wine which is the most important ceremony in the Christian Church. It remembers the Last Supper that Jesus ate with his disciples where he made the bread and wine symbols of his death. On that occasion Jesus gave thanks for the bread and wine before sharing it with his disciples. The word *eucharist* is a Greek word which means 'thanksgiving'. When Christians celebrate the Eucharist they are thanking God for all he has done for them.

The celebration of the Eucharist involves the blessing and eating of bread and wine (called the 'elements'), although the different denominations have their own beliefs about what happens during this act of worship.

> The various Christian denominations refer to this symbolic meal by different names.
>
> **Catholic Church**
> Eucharist or Mass
>
> **Church of Ireland and Methodist**
> Holy Communion
>
> **Baptist**
> The Lord's Supper or The Breaking of Bread
>
> **Presbyterian**
> The Lord's Supper or Communion

SYMBOLISM OF BREAD AND WINE

At the Last Supper Jesus took the symbols of the **Passover meal** and gave them new meaning.

As Passover celebrated the Covenant between God and his people, Jesus' death made a **New Covenant** between God and his people. That New Covenant is remembered in the Eucharist.

Passover remembers how God set the people free from slavery in Egypt. Christians celebrate how God has set them free from sin.

On the first Passover, God instructed the people to sacrifice a lamb. At the sign of its blood, death would 'pass over' and leave them unharmed. Christians believe that Christ's sacrifice means that they will not die, but have eternal life.

As the blood of a lamb sealed the **Old Covenant**, the blood of Jesus sealed the New Covenant. This is why Jesus is sometimes referred to as 'the lamb of God'.

The symbol of bread has layers of meaning:

- Bread is essential for life just as Jesus is essential for the Christian life. Jesus said *"I am the bread of life"* (John 6:35).

- Bread was the food of the poor and was easily available to all, just as Jesus is available to all who seek him with a sincere heart.

- In order for bread to be made the grain of wheat must be crushed, so bread becomes a powerful symbol of death and the sacrifice of Jesus' life.

- In the Eucharist the bread is broken, symbolising that Jesus body was physically broken.

The wine is also symbolic:

- At Passover, wine was a sign of God's blessing on His people. Jesus is God's blessing on His people.

- The colour of wine was an appropriate symbol of the blood that Jesus shed.

- In order for the wine to be made the grape must be crushed, so wine becomes a symbol of death and the sacrifice of Jesus' life.

TEACHER'S NOTE

For this section, those studying module 3.1 'The Christian Church through a study of the Catholic Church and One Protestant Tradition' should study the material on the Catholic Church and select one Protestant denomination.

Those studying module 3.2a 'The Christian Church with a focus on the Catholic Church' should study the material on the Catholic Church only.

Those studying module 3.2b 'The Christian Church with a focus on the Protestant Tradition' should study material on two Protestant denominations.
(Continue reading from page 110.)

THE SACRAMENT OF EUCHARIST IN THE CATHOLIC CHURCH

The service of Eucharist is usually called the **Mass**. Mass is celebrated every day in the Catholic Church and most Catholics attend Mass every Sunday. All Catholics who have been baptised and who have made the **Sacrament of Reconciliation** (confession) can receive the Eucharist. It is the central act of worship in the Catholic Church.

TRANSUBSTANTIATION

Catholics believe that the elements of bread and wine are transformed into the body and blood of Christ through the act of **consecration**. The Catholic Church teaches that:

> "… We know ourselves to be bound by the command the Lord gave on the eve of his Passion: 'Do this in remembrance of me.' We carry out this command of the Lord by celebrating the memorial of his sacrifice. In so doing we offer to the Father what he had given to us: the gifts of his creation, bread and wine, which by the power of the Holy Spirit and by the words of Christ, have become the body and blood of Christ. Christ is thus really and mysteriously made present."

BREAD ONLY

Unlike other Christian traditions, Catholics usually receive only the bread at Mass. There are a number of reasons for this:

- Catholics believe that once the bread and wine have been blessed the presence of Christ is in them. They should be treated as sacred. If someone drops a communion wafer it can be picked up, but this is not the case with spilled wine.

- In the crucifixion, Jesus' blood was separated from His body. At the Resurrection, his body and blood were no longer separate but one.

- When the bread and wine are consecrated they both become Christ. This means that when Catholics receive the bread they receive the whole Christ, body and blood.

- The priest receives both bread and wine (called 'Communion under both kinds').

CEREMONY OF THE EUCHARIST

- The people recall their sins and express sorrow for them in the **Penitential Rite**.

- The priest or a member of the congregation reads from the Bible in the **Liturgy of the Word**.

- The congregation say the **Creed** and the **Prayers of the Faithful**.

- If it is a Sunday, a collection of money will be taken, and offered up with the bread and wine in the offertory procession.

- The Priest will read the **Preface** and the **Eucharistic Prayer**. The central part of this is the Consecration of the bread and wine to become the body and blood of Christ.

- The **'Our Father'** is said followed by the **'Lamb of God'** prayer which emphasises Christ's sacrifice for the forgiveness of sins.

- The congregation process to the altar to receive the body and blood of Christ under the appearance of bread and wine. Usually, only the bread is distributed to the congregation.

- The priest ends the Mass with a blessing and a command to go out "to love and serve the Lord."

(The whole service is explored in more detail on page 46)

BELIEFS ABOUT MASS

IN A GROUP

Match up the following statements with the titles in the diagram (right:)

- Jesus commanded his disciples to *"Do this in memory of me"* at the last Supper. Christians obey this command.

- The mass brings the whole community together as well as bringing the believer and Christ into closer relationship.

- Catholics receive the body and blood of Christ under the appearance of bread and wine.

- *"Take this and eat. This is my body which is broken for you. Take this and drink. This is my blood which is poured out for you for the forgiveness of sins."*

- When Catholics celebrate the Mass they remember the words and actions of Jesus at the last Supper.

- The Mass is *eucharist*.

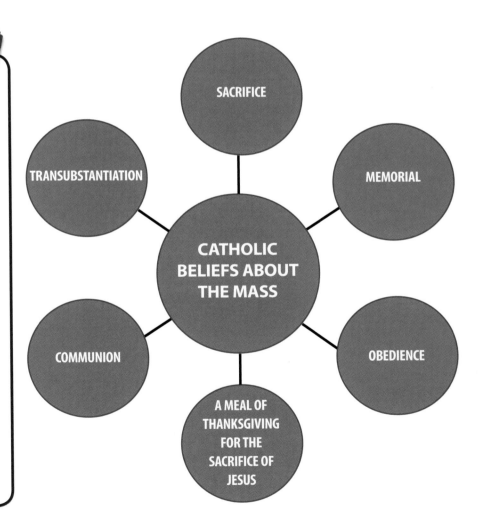

HOLY COMMUNION IN THE CHURCH OF IRELAND

In the Church of Ireland Holy Communion is celebrated on most Sundays. Communion is normally taken for the first time after Confirmation, usually at around 14 years old, when the individual decides to take on the baptismal vows for themselves.

A CEREMONY OF HOLY COMMUNION

- After greeting the congregation the rector says a preparation prayer (a **collect for purity**), which is followed by a hymn of praise.

- A member of the congregation will read from the Bible and then the rector will give the sermon.

- The congregation recites **the Apostles' Creed**.

- There are prayers of **intercession**, a reading of the commandments, prayers of **confession** and **absolution**.

- The **prayer of humble access** prepares people's hearts and minds to receive the sacrament.

- The congregation will share the **sign of peace**, shaking hands with each other and saying something like "The peace of the Lord be with you."

- An offering of money is taken to the altar where the bread and wine for communion are also placed.

- The rector takes the bread and wine in his hands and blesses them. He says a prayer of thanksgiving and the congregation respond by saying the **Lord's Prayer**.

- The rector breaks the bread and says "The bread which we break is a sharing in the body of Christ."

- The congregation replies with the words,

"We, being many, are one body for we all share in the one bread."

- The people move from their seats to kneel at the altar rail. The rector or his assistants put a small piece of bread into people's hands, and everyone takes a sip out of a common cup of wine.

- The rector says to each person "The body of Christ keep you in eternal life" and "The blood of Christ keep you in eternal life."

- There is a prayer of thanksgiving and commitment to serve Christ.

- The rector ends the service with a blessing: "Go in peace to love and serve the Lord." The congregation answers, "In the name of Christ. Amen."

WHAT DOES THE CHURCH OF IRELAND BELIEVE ABOUT HOLY COMMUNION?

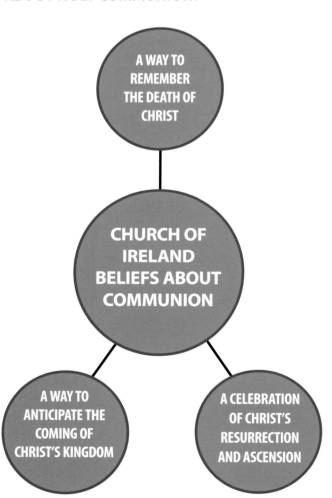

IN A GROUP

Match up the following explanations with the statements in the diagram to the left:

- During the celebration of Holy Communion Christians remember Jesus' death on the cross.

- Communion celebrates that Jesus rose from the dead and ascended into heaven.

- At communion Christians look forward to the Second Coming of Christ on Earth.

THE LORD'S SUPPER IN THE BAPTIST CHURCH

Baptists allow anyone who is a Christian to celebrate The Lord's Supper in their church. It does not matter what denomination they belong to or what age they are. The term for this is an **'open table'**.

Communion is usually celebrated once a week, at the end of the morning worship service, although in some Baptist Churches there is an evening celebration of the Lord's Supper once a month. It is a very informal time of sharing in the Baptist Church, although it is also considered to be a serious and reverent act of worship.

A CEREMONY OF THE LORD'S SUPPER

- After the morning worship service ends there is a time of quietness for people to think about the communion celebration they are about to participate in.

- The pastor will invite all present to share in an informal time of worship. Those present may choose a hymn or chorus for everyone to sing together.

- A member of the congregation may choose a Bible reading or pray to focus on the death and Resurrection of Christ.

- Someone will say a **prayer of thanks** for the bread.

- Then bread is passed around by **deacons** so that everyone present can take a piece. Once everyone has been served, they all eat their bread at the same time.

- The same procedure is carried out for the wine.

- A period of quietness follows for people to reflect.

- Finally the pastor prays and gives a **word of blessing**.

WHAT DO BAPTISTS BELIEVE ABOUT THE LORD'S SUPPER?

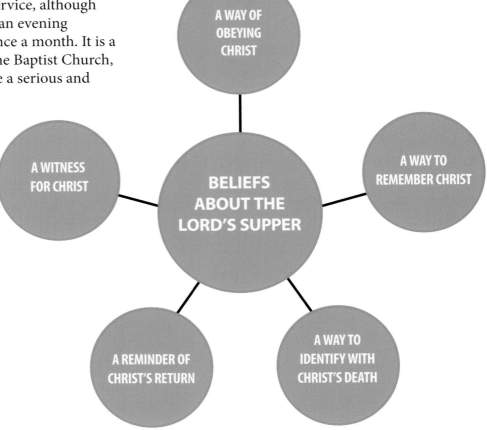

IN A GROUP

Match up the following explanations with the statements in the diagram on the previous page:

- At the Last Supper Jesus told his disciples *"Do this in remembrance of me"* (1 Corinthians 11:24). By celebrating the Lord's Supper Baptists believe they are obeying Christ.

- The bread and wine are symbols of Christ's body and blood. Baptists believe that the Lord's Supper is a memorial of the death of Christ on the cross.

- Baptists believe that when a person becomes a Christian they experience a death to their old, sinful way of life and that there is a spiritual rebirth or resurrection.

- By celebrating the Lord's Supper, Baptists believe that they are telling the world that they believe in Christ, that he died on the cross for the sin of the world and that through Christ's death there is salvation (being saved from sin).

- When Baptists celebrate communion they 'proclaim the Lord's death until he comes.' This refers to the belief in the Second Coming of Christ.

HOLY COMMUNION IN THE METHODIST CHURCH

Holy Communion is celebrated at least once a month in the Methodist church. It usually takes place during the worship service but can sometimes also occur in a more informal way, for example, at a Bible study.

Methodists allow anyone who is a Christian to celebrate Holy Communion in their church. It does not matter what denomination they belong to or what age they are. The term for this is an **'open table'**.

The minister will invite "those who love Him (the Lord) or who would like to love Him more" to participate in the celebration.

The wine used for communion is always non-alcoholic.

A CEREMONY OF HOLY COMMUNION

- Communion takes place following the **Ministry of the Word** (Bible readings and sermon).

- The congregation will recite the **Nicene Creed** together. This is to show that they are united with other churches.

- The congregation will **share the peace**, shaking hands with each other and saying something like "The peace of the Lord be with you."

- Cloths are removed from the bread and wine which are already on the communion table.

- The congregation says a **prayer of thanksgiving** for what Christ has done and to look forward to his return.

- The minister takes the bread, breaks it and invites the congregation to come forward, out of their seats, to receive the bread and wine.

- The people kneel at the communion rail and receive the elements of bread and wine from the minister and his stewards.

- When everyone has received communion the elements of bread and wine are covered up again by cloths and the people go back to their seats.

- The minister prays and, after a hymn, announces the **benediction** – a word of blessing.

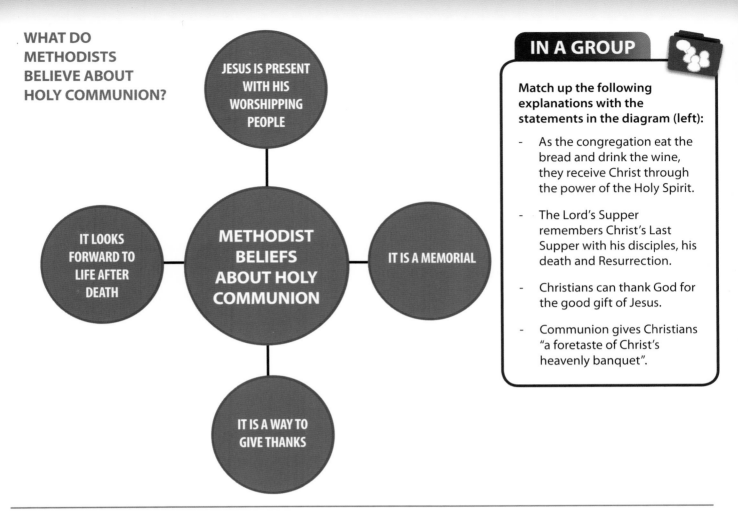

WHAT DO METHODISTS BELIEVE ABOUT HOLY COMMUNION?

JESUS IS PRESENT WITH HIS WORSHIPPING PEOPLE

IT LOOKS FORWARD TO LIFE AFTER DEATH

METHODIST BELIEFS ABOUT HOLY COMMUNION

IT IS A MEMORIAL

IT IS A WAY TO GIVE THANKS

IN A GROUP

Match up the following explanations with the statements in the diagram (left):

- As the congregation eat the bread and drink the wine, they receive Christ through the power of the Holy Spirit.

- The Lord's Supper remembers Christ's Last Supper with his disciples, his death and Resurrection.

- Christians can thank God for the good gift of Jesus.

- Communion gives Christians "a foretaste of Christ's heavenly banquet".

COMMUNION IN THE PRESBYTERIAN CHURCH

Communion is celebrated between two and six times a year in the Presbyterian Church. A pre-communion service is held on the Wednesday before Communion Sunday to help people to prepare for the sacrament. New church members are also formally welcomed at this service.

Anyone who professes to be a Christian is invited to celebrate communion in the Presbyterian Church. Children do not take communion. Teenagers who feel ready to celebrate the sacrament do so after a discussion with the minister and usually attend communion classes beforehand as well.

Presbyterians keep a record of those who take communion through the use of communion tokens. These little cards are filled out with each member's name and put into a basket on Communion Sunday. This is a useful record when it comes to times for the voting of new elders. It also can be used to provide information on who is no longer taking communion. The minister or elder may go to visit such people to make sure there are no problems.

A CEREMONY OF COMMUNION IN THE PRESBYTERIAN CHURCH

- Communion takes place in a normal Sunday service, morning or evening, after the sermon.

- The minister opens in prayer.

- The minister reads an appropriate passage from the New Testament, such as Matthew 26:27–29 or 1 Corinthians 11:23–25.

- The minister stands in front of the communion table and **prays a blessing** on the bread and wine.

- The bread and wine are given out to the congregation by elders.

- The bread is usually in small pieces or shortbread served on a plate that is passed around the pews.

- The wine is non-alcoholic, served in small individual glasses to each person.

- In some Presbyterian churches everyone waits until all people have been served and then take communion together.

- The minister says a **prayer of thanksgiving**.

- Everyone stands to sing a hymn.

- The service ends when the minister announces the **benediction** – a word of blessing.

WHAT DO PRESBYTERIANS BELIEVE ABOUT HOLY COMMUNION?

PRESBYTERIAN BELIEFS ABOUT HOLY COMMUNION

- ATONEMENT A way to identify with Christ's death.
- REMEMBRANCE
- THANKSGIVING
- NOURISHMENT
- TESTIMONY
- DEDICATION
- FELLOWSHIP AND SHARING
- EXPECTATION

IN A GROUP

Match up the following explanations with the statements in the diagram above:

- Communion helps Christians to remember the death of Christ.

- Christians have an opportunity to thank God and praise him for the death of Christ.

- By taking communion, the faith of Christians is built up.

- Christians take communion in the company of other believers and share in the fellowship of the Christian family.

- Communion is a way for Christians to renew their commitment to Christ.

- Christians look forward to the second coming of Christ.

- By taking communion Christians are declaring in a public way that they follow Christ.

FOR YOUR FOLDER

1. Describe the service of Communion/Eucharist in a denomination of your choice.

2. How does a communion service remind people about events in the life of Jesus?

3. What are some of the main differences in belief and practice of communion in the two denominations you have studied?

4. For what reasons do Christians take part in the act of Communion?

5. "You cannot celebrate Communion/Eucharist too often." Do you agree or disagree? Give reasons for your answer.

THE SACRAMENT OF CONFIRMATION IN THE CATHOLIC CHURCH

Confirmation is the third **Sacrament of Initiation** in the Catholic Church. When a believer has been confirmed then he or she is a **full member** of the Catholic Church.

In **Baptism** Catholics are first united with the Risen Jesus and become members of the Church.

In **Eucharist** Catholics become more closely united with the Risen Jesus and the Church when they receive the food of eternal life – the Body and blood of Jesus.

In **Confirmation** Catholics become full members of the Church and receive the fullness of the gifts of the Holy Spirit.

TEACHER'S NOTE

For this section, those studying module 3.1 'The Christian Church through a study of the Catholic Church and One Protestant Tradition' should study the material on the Catholic Church and select one Protestant denomination.

Those studying module 3.2a 'The Christian Church with a focus on the Catholic Church' should study the material on the Catholic Church only.

Those studying module 3.2b 'The Christian Church with a focus on the Protestant Tradition' should study the material on the Protestant Churches only.
(Continue reading from page 117.)

There is a close relationship between the Sacrament of Baptism and the Sacrament of Confirmation in the Catholic Church.

At Baptism Catholics first receive the Holy Spirit. At Confirmation they receive the fullness of the Holy Spirit.

At Baptism parents make baptismal promises on behalf of the child. At Confirmation the child renews those promises for themselves.

At Baptism the child is called to do the work of Christ. At Confirmation the child is strengthened by the Spirit to take on an adult role in the Church.

At Baptism Catholics first become members of the Church. At Confirmation they become full members of the Church.

At Baptism the child receives the love of God. At Confirmation the child is given the task of being witness to that love in the world.

PREPARING FOR CONFIRMATION

Preparation for the sacrament of Confirmation varies from parish to parish but will include the following:

- **Instruction** on the meaning of the sacrament and preparation for renewal of faith promises.
- **Meetings for parents** to remind them of the meaning and purpose of Confirmation. Parents renew their own confirmation promises and practical details such as giving a confirmation name, and the names of sponsors are worked out.
- **Sacrament of Reconciliation.** An opportunity is given for the young people to receive the Sacrament of Reconciliation before Confirmation.
- **Day of Preparation.** There is sometimes a whole day of rehearsal, including Mass.
- **The Confirmation Card** will include details of the confirmation name to be taken, place and date of baptism, and the name of sponsor.

WHO IS CONFIRMED IN THE CATHOLIC CHURCH?

Young people are usually confirmed in the Catholic Church when they are considered mature enough to understand the Sacrament and what it means. At 11 years old the young person is thought to have that maturity. Embarking on the journey through adolescence into adulthood is such a key moment and the Church marks it with this Sacrament, which will strengthen the young person in all the challenges that lie ahead by giving the gifts of the Holy Spirit.

THE CONFIRMATION CEREMONY IN THE CATHOLIC CHURCH

It is usually the bishop who administers the sacrament of Confirmation although in some circumstances he will delegate this to a priest. The sacrament of Confirmation usually takes place during Mass between the Liturgy of the Word and the Eucharist. The ceremony is structured as follows:

Presentation of the Candidate

The name of the candidate for Confirmation is read out from the Confirmation card and he or she stands up.

Renewal of Baptismal Promises

These take the form of question and answer, and are the same as those asked at baptism. The candidate renews those promises for themselves, making a personal commitment to the faith.

Laying on of Hands

The bishop raises his hands over those to be confirmed saying:

> *"Send down your Spirit upon them to be their helper and guide. Give then the spirit of wisdom and understanding, the spirit of right judgement and courage and the spirit of knowledge and reverence. Fill them with the spirit of wonder and awe in your presence".*

The laying on of hands is an ancient way of calling down the **power and blessing of God** upon someone. In the Old Testament it was a sign that someone had been **set apart for a special task. Power and strength** are being given to the candidate. **The Holy Spirit will come upon them in power and strength.**

The Anointing with Chrism

The candidate kneels. The name of the candidate and the new Confirmation name to be taken are read out from the Confirmation card. The Sponsor places their right hand on the shoulder of the candidate, the bishop anoints the candidate on the forehead with the chrism anointing oil making the sign of the cross.

> *"(Name) Be sealed with the gift of the Holy Spirit."*
> ***"Amen"***
> *"Peace be with you"*
> *"And also with you"*

The **oil of Chrism** is a symbol of being **set aside for a special task.** Oil is also a symbol of **healing** and **strengthening.** It will help the candidate meet all the challenges of the adult Christian life. The perfume of the oil is a symbol of the loving relationship between the Christian and God.

The **Confirmation name** is again symbolic of being given a **special task** to be **witness** to Christ

The **sign of the Cross** is a mark of God's ownership of the person

The **sign of peace** is symbolic of the Holy Spirit bringing the gift of peace and courage to the candidate.

Final blessing and dismissal

The Mass continues and with the Liturgy of the Eucharist. A special blessing is given at the end.

FOR YOUR FOLDER

1. Read over the ceremony of Confirmation again. Can you identify the seven gifts of Holy Spirit given to those who receive Confirmation?

   List them in a table and explain how you think they will help the Christian live out their Christian life.

2. Describe what happens during the ceremony of Confirmation in the Catholic Church.

3. Explain the meaning of the oil of chrism; the sign of the Cross; the sign of peace; the laying on of hands and the Confirmation name. How does each of these show the real meaning of the sacrament?

4. "A person is too young at 11 or 12 years old to receive the sacrament of Confirmation". Do you agree or disagree? Give reasons. Show that you have thought about another point of view.

CONFIRMATION AND CHURCH MEMBERSHIP IN THE PROTESTANT CHURCHES

Most churches have special services to mark people becoming church members for the first time. In churches that practice infant baptism, it is a chance for people who have grown up going to church to make a public declaration of faith for themselves. This often involves renewing the baptismal vows that were taken on their behalf when they were children. This is known as **confirmation.**

Usually, it is teenagers and young adults who are confirmed, but there is no set age for confirmation. Anyone may be confirmed who is old enough to answer responsibly for themselves. Many people are confirmed as adults.

NOTE

Laying on of hands

In the Bible we read that the apostles and other church leaders laid their hands on a Christian's head and prayed for them to receive the Holy Spirit (Acts 9:14–23 and 19:1–6). Today many churches still practice 'the laying on of hands' as a confirmation of faith. In Church of Ireland this happens in the Confirmation service, when the bishop lays his hands on the heads of the 'confirmation candidates'.

Preparation

Before people are confirmed they will usually go to a confirmation class. Here they will learn about the important beliefs of Christians and have an opportunity to discuss issues of faith and life with others. It is an important time for young Christians to learn about the commitment that being a Christian involves. They may have been baptised as a baby, but in the confirmation service they will make their own promises before God about choosing to live as a Christian and a member of the Church.

Different denominations believe different things about what happens in a service of confirmation:

- **Anglicans** believe that a person is confirmed by the Holy Spirit and strengthened to live a Christian life at confirmation.
- **Methodists** do not believe that any special change takes place through confirmation. However, during the service a prayer is said that the person will be blessed and that they will be established in the Holy Spirit.
- **Presbyterians** do not have services of confirmation, but there will be a special service for new members of the church to make a public statement of faith.
- **Baptists** do not practice confirmation. Instead, it is the act of Baptism by a young person or adult that declares their faith and willingness to follow Christ.

> **TEACHER'S NOTE**
>
> For this section you can study any or all of the denominations.

CONFIRMATION IN THE CHURCH OF IRELAND

In the Church of Ireland the bishop leads the service of confirmation. He explains how the Holy Spirit leads and guides Christians.

Some of the people being confirmed may explain to the congregation about why they want to follow Jesus and be confirmed. This is called a '**testimony**'.

The bishop asks the people being confirmed if they have been baptised. He asks them if they believe in Jesus and if they will try to live according to his teaching.

Each candidate for confirmation comes to the front in turn and kneels down. The bishop says:

> "'God has called you by name and made you his own."

The bishop puts his hand on their head and says:

> "Confirm, O Lord, your servant with your Holy Spirit."

They say:

> "Amen."

The bishop then draws the sign of the cross on the forehead of the candidate with anointing oil. Anointing with oil is an ancient sign of being chosen by God. The sign of the cross shows that the candidate is a child of God.

The newly confirmed Christians then receive communion with their friends, family and the rest of those present.

CONFIRMATION IN THE METHODIST CHURCH

The Methodist Church offers Christians the chance to show a step of commitment by being 'confirmed' and 'received into membership'. The confirmation service includes a renewal of baptismal promises and prayers for the work of the Holy Spirit in the person's life.

The minister lays their hands on the person's head and says:

> "Lord, confirm [strengthen] your servant (name) by your Holy Spirit that she/he may continue yours for ever."

In the same service, the person is '**received into membership**'. This means being welcomed into a particular Methodist church (usually their local church) which can support them in their faith and where they can support others. The person can participate in the life of the church by serving as a steward, pastoral visitor, church council member or local preacher.

In the service, the minister welcomes a person into membership saying:

> "We receive and welcome you as members of the Methodist Church, and of the church in this place."

The minister and a representative of the local church then shakes the hands of the new members.

At the Service of Confirmation and Reception into Membership two questions are asked as an affirmation of faith:

> "Do you turn away from evil and all that denies God?"

and

> "Do you turn to God, trusting in Jesus Christ as Lord and Saviour, and in the Holy Spirit as Helper and Guide?"

The answer to both questions is

> "By the grace of God I do."

After confirmation and the reception, the newly-confirmed are asked to make three promises:

> "Will you commit yourself to the Christian life of worship and service, and be open to the renewing power of God?"

> "Will you seek the strength of God's Spirit as you accept the cost of following Jesus Christ in your daily life?"

"Will you witness, by word and deed, to the good news of God in Christ, and so bring glory to God?'"

The response to each of these is:

"With God's help I will."

> The newly confirmed are reminded of what it means to be part of the Methodist Church:
>
> - Participating in worship in the local church, which includes regular sharing in Holy Communion, and personal prayer.
> - Learning through Bible study and fellowship meetings, so that they may grow in faith and support others in their discipleship.
> - Taking part in service in the community by being a good neighbour, challenging injustice and using their resources to support the Church in its mission in the world.
> - Evangelising, through working out their faith in daily life and sharing Christ with others.

MEMBERSHIP IN THE PRESBYTERIAN CHURCH

A person becomes a full member of the Presbyterian Church when they take communion for the first time – they become a '**communicant member**'. There is no age-limit for becoming a member, but it usually happens around 17–18 years.

To become a communicant member a person needs to go through preparation classes, however, it is not necessary to become a member to take communion. If a person wishes to become a member they need to speak to the minister a few months before the next communion service (remember communion only takes place between 4 and 6 times a year). The minister will usually make an announcement at the worship service to invite people to consider becoming communicant members if they have not already done so. If the response is strong there will be a series of preparation classes. Otherwise the minister will talk with potential members on a one-to-one basis.

The ceremony is called the **Reception of a Communicant**, and it takes place on the Wednesday evening before Communion Sunday. The new members meet with the Kirk Session (church elders) and one of them formally welcomes them into the church. Another elder prays for the new members. It is important that the new members show that they are committed Christians, so each of them makes a **public confession of their commitment** before the congregation.

This public declaration can take various forms. It can simply mean that the minister introduces them as coming before the congregation '**on profession of faith**'. In other churches they may be asked questions:

> *"Do you believe in one God, Father, Son and Holy Spirit and do you confess Jesus Christ as your Saviour and Lord?"*

> *"Do you promise to join regularly with your fellow Christians in worship on the Lord's Day?"*

> *"Do you promise to be faithful in the reading of the Bible and in prayer?"*

> *"Do you promise to give a fitting proportion of your time, talents and money for the Church's work in the world?"*

> *"Do you promise, depending on the grace of God, to confess Christ before men, to serve Him in your daily work, and to walk in His ways all the days of your life?"*

The person will answer *"yes"* to these questions and is now prepared to take communion and become a full member of the church.

MEMBERSHIP IN THE BAPTIST CHURCH

There are four requirements for becoming a member of the Baptist Church:

1. It is necessary to profess faith in Christ and repent of sin.
2. A person must show through their lives that they have been transformed or changed by Christ.
3. A person must be baptised (this can happen in the Baptist Church, but baptism in another denomination is usually also acceptable).
4. A person must agree with the doctrine of the Baptist Church.

To become a member it is necessary to apply in writing to the local Baptist Church. A person is then interviewed by two elders. At this interview the person will tell the story of how they became a Christian (this is sometimes called '**giving their testimony**'). After this there is a special meeting of the church where a report of any interviews is given. The applications for baptism must be accepted by a two-thirds majority vote of those present.

Following acceptance at the church meeting, a person is publicly received into membership of the church at the celebration of the Lord's Table on Sunday. The pastor gives the new member '**the right hand of fellowship**' (shaking hands) which is a sign of acceptance into the fellowship of the church (Galatians 2:9).

FOR YOUR FOLDER

1. Explain the meaning of a service of confirmation.
2. How is confirmation linked to baptism?
3. Do you think more importance should be given to confirmation in some denominations?

THE SACRAMENTS OF VOCATION IN THE CATHOLIC CHURCH

TEACHER'S NOTE

This section is for those studying module 3.2a 'The Christian Church with a focus on the Catholic Church'.

(Those studying module 3.1 or 3.2b should continue on to Chapter 7, page 129.)

MARRIAGE

In the Catholic Church, Baptism and Confirmation give a vocation or calling to live out the mission of the Church. However some Catholics may feel called to live out special vocations in marriage or in priesthood. The sacraments of vocation are Marriage and Holy Orders. The Catholic Church teaches that Marriage has four main principles:

- It is permanent (lifelong).
- It is life-giving (is for pro-creation).
- It is exclusive. Just as Christ's love for his people is faithful and unbroken so is the couple's love for each other.
- It is a Sacrament and a sign of Christ's love for his Church. The grace of God has been given to the couple. As other sacraments are unbreakable so marriage is unbreakable.

These beliefs about marriage influence what the Church teaches about divorce and family planning (contraception).

Preparation for Marriage

Because of the seriousness of the commitment made by couples in marriage most Catholic diocese require that couples complete a pre-marriage course. These help couples to:

- reflect on what marriage involves.
- gain from the experience of other married couples who facilitate the course.
- discuss practical issues like the management of household chores, financial management, etc.
- focus on the expectations they each have from marriage.

FOR YOUR FOLDER

What advantages might there be to attending marriage preparation classes?

ANNULMENT

An annulment can be granted to a couple by the Church when it shown that one or both partners did not **freely and fully consent** to the first three of the principles of marriage listed above. Annulment may also be granted if the marriage was **not sacramental**, if the couple's consent was not witnessed and blessed by a Catholic priest. A marriage is not considered valid if it is not **consummated** by sexual intercourse.

An annulment is not the same as a divorce. An annulment means the marriage is null and void. In other words, as far as the Catholic Church is concerned, a valid marriage has not taken place to begin with.

The Church teaches that there may be **impediments** to marriage (something that stops full and free consent being given). These impediments may include:

- Social or emotional pressure put on either partner to marry.
- Illness or addiction which may have impacted on the understanding or judgement of either partner.
- Infidelity at the time of the marriage.

FOR YOUR FOLDER

Test your understanding. Read the examples below and discuss which couples may not have a valid marriage. Give reasons for your answers.

Paul and Jane have been together for two years. They are both 18 years old. Jane is unsure if Paul really is the right person for her. Jane becomes pregnant. Both parents want to make sure that their grandchild is born into wedlock. They work hard on persuading the couple they could make a marriage work. Despite her doubts Jane agrees. She does not want to disappoint her parents further.

Sam and Fiona have been married for 10 years and have 2 children. They were happy together until Fiona met someone at work and began to have an affair with him. Sam would have forgiven her but Fiona says she wants to be with the other man. She takes the children and leaves Sam.

Simon and Amy are about to get married in two weeks time. Simon doesn't mind the idea of getting married but he really doesn't want to have children. Amy has been talking more and more about when they would have their first baby and how many children they will have. He tries to sound non-committal about it all. He is sure he can persuade her to his way of thinking when they marry but he can't tell her now so close to the wedding ...

WHAT DOES THE CATHOLIC CHURCH TEACH ABOUT DIVORCE?

Because of the Catholic understanding of marriage as a solemn sacrament, the Catholic Church does not accept divorce.

- As with other sacraments, marriage cannot be undone.

- The Church finds support for its teaching in several places in scripture. For example, in Matthew 19:3–12 Jesus makes his teaching on divorce very clear.

- The Catholic Church believes divorce is wrong because of the destruction and hurt it causes, especially to children who are often traumatised and feel torn between two parents.

The Church teaches that:

"Divorce is a grave offence against the natural law. It claims to break the contact, to which the spouses freely consent, to live with each other until death ... Contracting a new union, even if it recognised by civil law, adds to the gravity of the rupture ..."

CCC (2384)

SEPARATION

This is when the husband and wife are not divorced, but no longer live together. A couple may be legally separated or informally separated by mutual agreement. The Church recognises that this might sometimes be a necessary step for a couple in order to solve or ease the difficulties they are having.

"We must reach out with love – the love of Christ – to those who know the pain of failure in marriage; to those who know the loneliness of bringing up a family on their own; to those whose family life is dominated by tragedy or by illness of mind or body."

Pope John Paul II, May 31st 1982 in York

IN A GROUP

Look up the bible references below and compile a list of reasons why the Catholic Church does not permit divorce on the grounds of Scripture.

Matthew 19:3–12

Matthew 5:27–30

Matthew 5:31–32

John 8:1–11

1 Corinthians 7: 10–11.

How does the Catholic understanding of marriage influence the Church's teaching on divorce?

FOR YOUR FOLDER

1. Explain why the Catholic Church teaches that divorce is wrong.
2. What is adultery?
3. Why would Christians condemn adultery?

FURTHER THINKING

Find out what help and support the Catholic Church offers to couples who are experiencing marital difficulties.

THE CATHOLIC CHURCH AND CONTRACEPTION

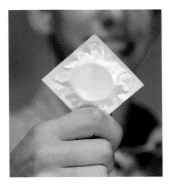

The official teaching of the Catholic Church is that artificial forms of contraception, such as condoms, should not be used.

- In the marriage ceremony the couple promise to accept lovingly any children that God will give. This means that every act of sexual intercourse between the husband and wife should be open to the conception of a new life.

- In Genesis 1:28, God commissions the man and woman: *"Have many children, so that your descendants will live all over the earth and bring it under their control"*. The Catholic Church teaches that a husband and wife should not artificially interfere with God's plan for marriage in any way.

- The Church understands the act of sexual love as an expression of the love of husband and wife, but it is also the source of new human life.

- Catholic couples are not discouraged from thinking about and planning how many children they would like to have, but there are natural means of doing this. The Catholic Church teaches against artificial contraception.

THE MARRIAGE CEREMONY IN THE CATHOLIC CHURCH

The Rite of Marriage usually takes place during Mass between the Homily and the Liturgy of the Eucharist. Occasionally, the Rite of Marriage is celebrated on its own without a Mass.

- **The Greeting.** The bride and groom are welcomed by the priest.

- **The Homily.** The priest will usually explain the meaning and importance of the sacrament of marriage.

- **The Questioning and Consent.** This is an important way of making sure that both the bride and the groom understand the seriousness of the responsibilities they are about to undertake in marriage. The questioning reflects the Catholic understanding of the sacrament of marriage.

*"Have you come to give yourself to each other **freely and without reservation?"***

*"Will you love and honour each other **for life?"***

*'Will you accept **children** lovingly from God?'*

- **The Vows.** This is the actual moment that the sacrament of marriage is given. The couple make the marriage vows to each other saying:

*"I (name) do take thee (name) to be my lawful wedded wife/husband, to have and to hold from this day forward, for better for worse, for richer for poorer, in sickness and in health, to love and to cherish, **till death us do part***".

- **Acceptance of Consent and Blessing.** The priest accepts the bride and groom's consent to give the sacrament of marriage to one another. He represents the Church and calls down the blessing of God on the consent and marriage of the couple. For this reason a priest must be present at a Catholic marriage.

The priest says:

*"You have declared your consent before the Church. May the Lord in His goodness, strengthen your consent and fill you both with His blessings. **What God had joined together, let no man put asunder***"

- **Exchange of rings.** The priest blesses the rings:

*"May the Lord bless these rings which you give to each other as a sign of your **love** and **fidelity***"

The couple exchange rings saying:

"Take this ring as a sign of my love and fidelity in the name of the Father and of the Son and of the Holy Spirit."

- **The Nuptial Blessing.** If there is a wedding Mass this blessing is given after the Our Father. The blessing emphasises that:

  - the couple's love for each other is a reflection of the love God has for His people and is therefore to be unbroken.

  - marriage is a sign of that faithful love for all people to see.

Civil law requires that the marriage be registered. So the register is signed and the certificate is given. The priest is an authorised registrar.

FOR YOUR FOLDER

1. Read through the ceremony carefully. Show how the Catholic marriage ceremony reflects Catholic teaching on marriage. The excerpts in **bold** will help you.

2. In what way do you think the ring is a sign of the fidelity and permanence of marriage?

HOLY ORDERS

The Sacrament of Holy Orders is given to men who are called to be priests.

WHO CAN RECEIVE THE SACRAMENT OF HOLY ORDERS?

- Men who have a strong desire to be a priest.

- Men who have a character that is suitable to meet the demands of priesthood (look back to page 34 to refresh your memory on the role of the priest).

- Men who are capable of the seven years of study required to be priest.

- Men who have been recommended for the priesthood by a bishop.

THE CEREMONY OF ORDINATION (HOLY ORDERS)

Ordination takes place during Mass between the Liturgy of the word and the Liturgy of the Eucharist. It commences after the Homily given by the bishop. Many other clergy attend and take part in the Ordination but the bishop is the one who confers the Sacrament.

Presentation of Candidate

The candidate is presented to the bishop who explains in a homily what the role of priest entails.

This is in the form of a series of questions and answers.

> *"Will you fulfil the office of a priest ... to care for God's people?"*

> *"Will you celebrate the sacraments faithfully?"*

> *"Will you preach the Gospel and explain the Catholic faith?"*

> *"Will you consecrate your life to God for the salvation of His people?"*

The candidate places his hands between the two hands of the bishop – an ancient sign of obedience and makes a promise of obedience to the bishop.

> *"Do you promise respect and obedience to me and my successors?"*

The candidate replies:

> *"I do"*

The bishop says:

> *"May God who has begun the good work in you bring it to fulfilment"*

There is a litany to the saints asking their prayers for the candidate.

The actual ordination now takes place. The bishop lays his hands on the head of the candidate who kneels down. All the priests taking part do the same in silence. The bishop then says a prayer while the participating priests stand in semi-circle around the candidate:

> *"Almighty Father, grant to this servant of yours the dignity of the priesthood ... may he be faithful to the ministry he received from you ... and be a model of right conduct."*

The Investiture

The stole is placed around the neck of the priest and he puts on the Mass vestments for the first time.

Anointing of hands

The bishop anoints the priests hands with chrism and prays that the priest will persevere in all his duties.

Presentation of the gifts

When the gifts are brought to the bishop in the Offertory procession he gives them to the newly ordained priest who will consecrate the bread and wine for the first time.

Sign of peace

The ceremony ends with the bishop offering the sign of peace to the new priest. The other priests participating do the same as a sign of welcome.

FOR YOUR FOLDER

1. Identify the main symbols in the Sacrament of Ordination.

2. Which of the symbols are used in other sacraments?

3. What do you think they mean in this sacrament?

4. Why do you think the priest makes the promise of obedience?

5. How do you think receiving the Sacrament of Ordination prepares the priest for his ministry? (Look at pages 34–35 again if you need to refresh your memory).

IN A GROUP

Some Catholics live out their vocation as a lay person, some as priests, some as religious sisters, brothers or nuns.

Think of different ways that lay people can live out their vocation in the Christian Church.

For example:

• By creating a loving home for children and bringing them up in the faith by teaching and example.

• Bringing God's word to others by reading at Mass

Religious Orders

Some feel a vocation to join a Religious order or Congregation. They live in Community together and take vows of poverty, chastity and obedience. The people who are called to these religious vocations take vows but do not receive a sacrament to mark their vocation.

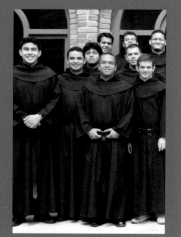

FURTHER THINKING

Use the internet or a library to find out more about religious orders, the vows they take and the work they do.

Can you find out the difference between an apostolic and a contemplative religious order?

SACRAMENTS OF HEALING IN THE CATHOLIC CHURCH

There are two sacraments of healing in the Catholic Church. These are the **Sacrament of Reconciliation** and the **Sacrament of the Sick**.

THE SACRAMENT OF RECONCILIATION

The Sacrament of Reconciliation is the means by which God extends his forgiveness to the believer when they approach the priest (the representative of Jesus) in sorrow for their sin.

The sacrament can be celebrated in different ways:

• As an individual celebration between the penitent and the priest. This is commonly known as '**confession**'. In some churches people may choose whether to confess in an individual confession box or in an 'open' confessional.

- There may be a community Penitential Service with individual confessions. A whole service including scripture readings and reflections to help people to examine their conscience takes place then people confess individually. This type of service reminds people that their sin hurts other people.

- There may be a community service where general absolution is given without individual confession. Special permission for this type of service is given from the bishop. It may be used when there is a shortage of priests to celebrate the sacrament to the extent that people would have to go without the sacrament for a long time.

THE CEREMONY FOR THE SACRAMENT OF RECONCILIATION

A 'Confessional Booth' where the sacrament of reconciliation is often given.

- **Greeting** – the priest welcomes the penitent.

- **Scripture reading** – a short excerpt from Scripture is shared on the theme of God's mercy and forgiveness.

- **Confession of sin** – the penitent confesses their sins with help from the priest to make a thorough Confession. The priest gives advice to the penitent on how to overcome their weaknesses and live a better life.

> **NOTE**
> Someone coming to receive the Sacrament of Reconciliation is called a 'penitent'.

- **Penance is given** – the priest suggests a 'penance' to help the penitent live a better life. This might be prayer or an act of charity such as giving to the poor.

- **Act of Contrition** – said by the penitent to show sorrow for sin.

- **Absolution** – the priest extends his right hand or both hands over the penitent and says:

  "I absolve you from your sins in the name of the Father and of the Son and of the Holy Spirit."

  He also says the Prayer of Absolution over the penitent.

- **Prayer of Praise and final blessing** – the priest tells the penitent to *"Go in Peace"*.

THE SACRAMENT OF ANOINTING OF THE SICK

Laying hands on sick people for God's healing has always been a practice of the Christian Church.

> *"Are any of you ill? You should send for the church elders, who will pray for them and rub olive oil on them in the name of the Lord. This prayer made in faith will heal the sick; the Lord will restore them to health, and the sins they have committed will be forgiven."*
>
> James 5:14–15

> **NOTE**
> The sacrament of the Anointing of the Sick is not the same as 'The Last Rites' or Extreme Unction. These are reserved for those who are dying .The Sacrament of the Sick can be received more than once. It often gives comfort and is spiritually strengthening to those who are sick.

WHO RECEIVES THE SACRAMENT OF THE SICK?

- Those who are dangerously ill.
- Someone who is about to have surgery.
- The weak and elderly.
- Sick children.
- Those who are unconscious but would have wanted to receive the sacrament.

THE CEREMONY FOR THE ANOINTING OF THE SICK

- **Greeting** –the priest will greet the sick person, sprinkle holy water upon them and explain the Sacrament to them.

THE CEREMONY FOR THE ANOINTING OF THE SICK

- **Greeting** – the priest will greet the sick person, sprinkle holy water upon them and explain the Sacrament to them.

- **Confession** – the sick person may confess their sins.

- **Scripture Reading** – the priest may also give a short homily or explanation.

- **Prayers of Intercession** – for the intercession of the saints for the sick person and those who care for them.

- **Laying on of hands**

  - **Prayer of Thanksgiving or blessing of the oil** – the priest will either say a prayer of thanks for the oil blessed on Holy Thursday or bless some olive oil.

  - **Anointing** –the person who is ill is anointed on the forehead and hands with the words:

  "Through this Holy Anointing may the Lord in His love and mercy help you with the grace of the Holy Spirit. May the Lord who saves you from sin, save you and raise you up."

- **Prayer After the Anointing**

- **The Our Father**

FOR YOUR FOLDER

1. Identify the words said in the anointing of a sick person.

2. Explain the effect receiving the sacrament might have on the person who is sick.

3. What do you think the laying on of hands symbolises?

4. What are the differences and similarities between the two sacraments of healing?

Chapter 7

THE ROLE OF THE CHURCH IN CONTEMPORARY SOCIETY

THE CONTRIBUTION OF THE CHRISTIAN CHURCHES TO PEACE AND RECONCILIATION IN A DIVIDED SOCIETY

Northern Ireland could be described as a 'divided society' in terms of both religion and politics. Christianity is the main religion in Northern Ireland but there is a history of division and conflict between groups of Catholics and Protestants. Similarly in politics there has been considerable conflict between Unionists (those supporting union with Britain) and Nationalists (those in favour of a United Ireland). Many of you will be used to seeing territorial markings such as painted kerbstones and the flying of national flags.

Over the years, churches in Northern Ireland have made a substantial contribution to reconciliation between the Protestant and Catholic communities.

IN A GROUP

1. What do you know about the period of history in Northern Ireland that is referred to as 'The Troubles'?

2. Have you ever taken part in cross-community projects?

FURTHER THINKING

Find out about cross-community projects in your school, church or area.

THE CORRYMEELA COMMUNITY

The Corrymeela Community was founded in 1965 by the Rev. Ray Davey, chaplain at Queen's University, Belfast. The community is a group of Christians in Ireland, both Protestant and Catholic, who believe they are called together as the 'Instrument of God's Peace' in the Church and the world. Corrymeela was set up to encourage reconciliation and peace-building in Northern Ireland, through the healing of social, religious and political divisions.

Throughout the period known as 'The Troubles', the Corrymeela Community worked with individuals and communities that suffered through violence and division caused by the Northern Irish conflict. It continues to encourage positive relationships between all kinds of people by:

- providing a safe place for people to express themselves.

- providing the opportunity for dialogue between people from contrasting religious traditions.

- supporting victims of violence and injustice.

CORRYMEELA: PROJECTS AND ACTIVITIES

Corrymeela runs three centres in Belfast, Ballycastle, and Glenshesk.

Corrymeela Centre, Ballycastle

The centre has facilities for over 100 residents allowing people the chance to stay and enjoy picturesque surroundings while participating in programmes:

- Work with schools focuses on community relations issues, often through citizenship.
- Family work.
- Work with church communities, in their own faith, and to support meeting people from other religious traditions.
- Youth work, primarily focused on marginalised young people (those who are outsiders).
- Community work looking at issues of inter-community relations, and cross-community work.
- Sanctuary and support for victims and those under stress.
- 'Treetops' children's bereavement support group.

Knocklayd

Situated on the slopes of Knocklayd Mountain in Antrim, this centre offers a place of retreat and respite for groups of up to 16 while encouraging 'ecumenical spirituality'.

Corrymeela House, Belfast

Corrymeela House functions as an administrative office and meeting place for Corrymeela groups in the city.

NOTE

'ECUMENICAL' – promoting unity between different Christian denominations.

FOR YOUR FOLDER

1. What is the Corrymeela Community?
2. Explain how the Corrymeela Community encourages positive relationships between all kinds of people.
3. Give four examples of the work carried out at the Corrymeela centres.
4. Do you think that the kind of cross-community relationships developed at Corrymeela are valuable? Give reasons for your answer.

FURTHER THINKING

Find out about some of the personal stories from people who have been helped by the Corrymeela Community from their website: www.corrymeela.org

The Advantages of Cross-Community projects:

- It provides a platform for re-examining the differences that have divided Christians and created mistrust.

- Honest and open discussion of all areas of faith are encouraged. Christians learn **to disagree without being disagreeable.**

- People can gradually learn about the other tradition, its spiritual strengths and weaknesses.

- **Strangers become friends** People can socialise together and enjoy each other's culture.

- Protestants and Catholics realise how important Christ is in each other's faith-tradition; and discover just how much truth they have **in common**.

- Christians can be united in worship.

- It shows other congregations of the Church, Catholic and Protestant, the value of such contact between the two traditions.

FURTHER THINKING

You can find out about the work of The Cornerstone Community from their website: www.cornerstonecommunity.co.uk

IN A GROUP

Copy and complete the table by looking up the verses and explaining the relevance of the teaching for reconciliation:

Biblical Teaching	Teaching for today
Galatians 3:28	Most Christians today would say that this means there is no difference between Catholic or Protestant, black or white, man or woman, settled person or traveller.
Acts 17:26	
Matthew 22:39	
Genesis 1:26–27	

THE CONTRIBUTION OF THE CHRISTIAN CHURCH TO LOCAL COMMUNITY AND COMMUNITY COHESION

We have seen how religious differences have caused social division in the past; however, many churches and Christian groups work to bring the community together and create cohesion. The word '**cohesion**' means 'holding together'.

In the past, when more people attended church services, the local church was often the heart of the community. In some places, social and community life still revolves around the church. The Church is a community of people and they aim to spread the benefits of that community to those around them. This is often referred to as '**outreach**'.

Outreach can simply mean that individual Christians aim to form good relationships with people they meet, but churches and other Christian groups can organise events and activities that benefit the wider community around them.

For example:

- **Youth work**

  Most churches have some form of organised youth work such as Youth Clubs, Scouts and Guides, Boy's Brigade and Girl's Brigade, football clubs, drop-in centres and Church Schools.

- ## Clubs and societies

  Some churches run a wide range of clubs and societies as varied as bowling, photography, flower-arranging, film nights, painting classes and discussion groups. These are open to anyone, and aim to create community cohesion and good relationships.

- ## Support groups

  Depending on the resources available to them, some local churches are able to offer free professional support and advice such as family planning or counselling, and run groups like Alcoholics Anonymous.

- ## Worship Services

  Sunday Morning services create community cohesion as people worship together and become part of a church family. Most churches make efforts to make the service as accessible and welcoming as possible for newcomers.

- ## Supporting other projects

  Some churches offer practical help to other organisations that work in the community like homeless shelters or care programmes.

CHURCH PROJECTS

Embrace NI

Embrace NI is a group of Christians who have come together to support asylum seekers and refugees in Northern Ireland, particularly those who are homeless or are out of work. Some churches support its work by collecting clothes and toiletries for distribution. Others work for the organisation providing information, training and resources to encourage church communities to welcome people from minority ethnic backgrounds.

Interfaith

Ireland has become a multi-faith island. Christians live alongside Muslims, Hindus, Jews, Buddhists, Humanists and others. Many denominations, for example the Methodist Church, believe it is important "to befriend, to include in community life and to journey along with those whose faith is not Christian"

Irish Methodism and Inter-Faith Understanding; Report to Conference 2007

Storehouse

Storehouse is a project to provide food parcels for struggling families across Belfast. People can donate food and volunteer to help packing in the warehouse or distributing the food. The project was started by Belfast City Vineyard, and a number of other local churches soon got involved.

Nightlight

Nightlight is an outreach project run by the Presbyterian Church. On the busy streets of Belfast every Friday and Saturday night, volunteers spend time giving out tea, talking, and offering practical help to partygoers and the homeless.

SVP

The Catholic charity 'The Society of St Vincent de Paul' is the largest, voluntary, charitable organisation in Ireland. It has been helping to alleviate poverty and work for social justice in Northern Ireland since 1848. The aim of the Society is: "to enhance the quality of life for those in need, regardless of creed, colour or caste".

Volunteers offer friendship, support, advice and practical help to families, pensioners and individuals each week. Some examples of the services offered by St Vincent de Paul include:

- Cash assistance
- Food and clothing
- Shops and internet cafés
- Furniture Stores
- Breakfast and Afterschool clubs
- Crèche
- Playgroup
- Mother and Toddler Group
- Centre for the Deaf (Belfast)
- Drop-in centres
- Resource centres
- Providing accommodation to vulnerable people
- Holiday schemes
- Holiday Home (Newcastle)

With 179 branches across Northern Ireland, individuals can get involved as volunteers. Churches, clubs and schools can help by fundraising with bake sales, auctions, sponsored sports days or whatever they can come up with.

Laura, Debbie and Bronagh from the St Vincent de Paul Conference at Our Lady and St Patrick's College, Belfast on visitation work.

FOR YOUR FOLDER

1. What is the aim of the St Vincent de Paul Society?
2. Give four examples of the kind of work they do.

IN A GROUP

1. How might churches develop ways of reaching out to teenagers and young adults in the community?

2. How can church buildings make a contribution to the life of the local community?

3. What do you think are the main problems facing Christians who want to witness to people on the streets at night?

4. "Christians have nothing to offer young people who just want to go out and have a good time on a Saturday night." Do you agree or disagree? Give reasons for your answer showing you have looked at contrasting points of view.

COMMUNITY SERVICE

One of the ways that Christian schools seek to contribute to community cohesion is through community service programmes.

Dominic explains: "School is about developing the whole person and not just dealing with the academic side of life. Being involved in community service stimulates the students' awareness of the other person's situation and needs, and encourages them to think of a practical response. It also helps develop their sense of empathy.

Community service can sow a seed for later life in appreciating the value of working with others in their wider community who may benefit from their help and friendship.

From a religious faith point of view it enables the young person to fulfill their apostolic calling to put Christian values into action."

Rachel, Maeve and Hannah, Students from Our Lady and St Patrick's College, Belfast, are involved in community service in the area in which their school is situated. They give up an hour and a half of their own time each week to carry out community service work with 13–17 year olds who have learning difficulties.

Hannah says:

"We had seen older students going out on community service over the years and the satisfaction and enjoyment they got from it. I wanted to be part of it. I work with students who are my own age and I always get a sense of the things I can do which they can't and I feel grateful."

Maeve says:

"It is great to see the joy and excitement in the eyes of the children when we visit. The work is really rewarding. It is a pity we only have an hour and a half every week. I would love to stay longer."

Although the community service programme ends in April. Many people choose to continue their service. I can see why."

Rachel says:

"I didn't know that there were people with special needs so close to the school. I think it is important to give something back to the local community and to become more involved – particularly with people who are less fortunate."

Rachel, Maeve and Hannah were so struck by the needs of the students and the skill and dedication of the teachers at Torbank school that they, led by Maeve, organised a sponsored walk to raise money for equipment . They raised £1000.

IN A GROUP

Make a list of the benefits of being involved in community service.

THE CHALLENGE TO THE CHRISTIAN CHURCH OF CHANGING MORAL, SOCIAL AND CULTURAL VALUES

One of the biggest challenges facing the Christian Church in the twenty-first century is its attitude to changing moral, social and cultural values. Attitudes towards issues such as sex before marriage, divorce, abortion, euthanasia and war have all faced change in society. This is a major challenge to the Christian Church, which often sees itself having a responsibility to set a moral example in the world.

Christians try to live according to God's standards and the teachings of Jesus, and look to the Bible for guidance on moral issues. However, many of the issues that are controversial today are not directly mentioned in the Bible. It is up to the Church to interpret the Bible and to apply its teachings to today's moral issues.

Many Christians accept the traditional opinions of the Church regarding most moral, social and cultural values. Others argue that the Church needs to move with the times. They believe the time has come for the Church to re-evaluate its opinion on the issues that cause most debate in today's world.

Three issues that cause controversy in the Church today are abortion, euthanasia and homosexuality.

IN A GROUP

"Society's values are moving further away from Biblical ideals."

Do you agree or disagree? Give reasons for your answer.

THE ISSUE OF ABORTION

Many different groups and organisations are debating the rights and wrongs of abortion.

One of the main ethical debates has been about the point at which life begins. When does a group of growing cells count as a human being? Does life begin at conception or birth?

The churches all agree that life begins in the womb, however, they differ on whether or not abortion is ever acceptable. Look at the following church statements:

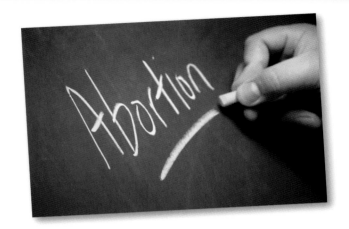

Denomination	Statement on Abortion
Catholic Church	*"Life must be respected with the utmost care from the moment of conception. Abortion and infanticide are abominable crimes."* Gaudium et Spes 51:3
Anglican **(Church of Ireland)**	The Lambeth conference of 1958 received a Committee Report in which it was stated: *"In the strongest terms, Christians reject the practice of induced abortion, or infanticide, which involves the killing of a life already conceived (as well as a violation of the personality of the mother) save at the dictate of strict and undeniable medical necessity."*
Presbyterian Church	*"The scriptures leave us in no doubt that from his earliest days in the womb, the unborn child is fully human, a person made in the image of God."* Leaflet on Abortion, p.1
Methodist Church	From The Status of the Unborn, a report received by the Methodist Conference 1992: *"The worth of the human race itself hinges on reverence for human life at every stage and the long tradition of Christian teaching is marked by an abhorrence of destroying the life in the womb. But a right to life does not mean an absolute right. Other lives have impinging rights. The life of the mother, whose survival may be crucial because care for the existing family heavily depend upon her, would appear to have priority over that of the foetus, if a choice has to be made …"*

FOR YOUR FOLDER

Create a table summarising the attitude of each denomination to abortion based on the information above.

THE ISSUE OF EUTHANASIA

Euthanasia is sometimes known as 'mercy killing' and it refers to the ending of someone's life. It can take the form of actively ending life, such as lethal injections, or simply withholding life-support or medication. One form of Euthanasia, known as 'assisted suicide', has become quite prominent in the media.

Recently, there has been debate about whether all forms of Euthanasia should be illegal and whether people have the right to choose to die, or to request that others end their life.

Many churches have released statements on their position:

Denomination	Statement on Euthanasia
Catholic Church	*"It is necessary to state firmly once more that nothing and no one can in any way permit the killing of an innocent human being, whether a fetus or an embryo, an infant or an adult, an old person, or one suffering from an incurable disease, or a person who is dying. Furthermore, no one is permitted to ask for this act of killing, either for himself or herself or for another person entrusted to his or her care, nor can he or she consent to it, either explicitly or implicitly … What a sick person needs, besides medical care, is love, the human and supernatural warmth with which the sick person can and ought to be surrounded by all those close to him or her, parents and children, doctors and nurses."* Declaration on Euthanasia, Sacred Congregation for the Doctrine of the Faith, 1980
Presbyterian Church	*"Compassion for our fellow human beings means we have the duty to help them die in as comfortable and peaceful ways as we can. We also believe that death is not disaster for those who have committed their lives to Christ. Dying in faith means going to be with him and it is right that we should welcome the release of death for those whose quality of life has been reduced to a daily grind of suffering or infirmity … Above all, the Christian community should take the lead in showing the prayerful, dignified, respectful care which assures people that they are valued and loved, even in the midst of pain and helplessness".* Social Issues & Resources Committee
Anglican (**Church of Ireland**)	*"… I am not arguing in favour of prolonged suffering … one of the most terrible things that can happen to us, as human beings, is to watch someone we love go through suffering … we can see, at first glance, the reasons why, if someone is suffering terribly with a terminal illness, we might consider euthanasia to be a desirable option …What is needed is not what some are calling, in a horrible travesty of language, the 'therapeutic option' of euthanasia or assisted suicide, but far greater resource – for greater training in palliative care, a care which embraces body, mind and soul."* The Bishop of St Albans, Christopher Herbert, commenting in opposition to the Assisted Dying Bill, 2005

FOR YOUR FOLDER

1. Based on the information in the table (left), place the Catholic, Presbyterian and Anglican Churches on the scale below.

   Attitude to Euthanasia

   Always Wrong Always Acceptable

2. Based on the table select a short quotation for each of the Churches, summarising their attitude to euthanasia.

IN A GROUP

1. Explain why the issue of euthanasia causes controversy for the Christian Church.

2. Which denominations are totally against euthanasia?

3. Do you imagine that there will ever be a change of attitude regarding euthanasia among the leadership of these churches?

FURTHER THINKING

What can you find out about the Methodist Church's attitude to euthanasia?

THE ISSUE OF HOMOSEXUALITY

Attitudes to homosexuality have varied throughout history and across culture. Christians aim to base their attitudes and understandings on God's teaching, rather than on the attitudes of those around them, but there is debate on what the Church should teach about homosexuality and about the place in the Church of people in homosexual relationships.

Look at the statements below:

Denomination	Statement on Homosexuality
Catholic Church	*"Homosexuality refers to relations between men or between women who experience an exclusive or predominant sexual attraction toward persons of the same sex. … Its psychological genesis remains largely unexplained. Basing itself on Sacred Scripture, which presents homosexual acts as acts of grave depravity, tradition has always declared that 'homosexual acts are intrinsically disordered' … Under no circumstances can they be approved … men and women who have deep-seated homosexual tendencies … must be accepted with respect, compassion, and sensitivity. Every sign of unjust discrimination in their regard should be avoided …"* The Catechism of the Catholic Church
Anglican **(Church of Ireland)**	• *A resolution was passed at the Lambeth Conference in 1998, stating that homosexual acts are 'incompatible with Scripture'. However, it also said this policy would not be the final word.* • *In 2003, the Church of England was prepared to appoint as bishop, Jeffrey John, a priest living in a celibate domestic partnership with another man. Many Anglicans were outraged and the priest decided not to accept the appointment.* • *Many Church of Ireland parishes are opposed to homosexual practice, while others have openly gay parishioners.*
Presbyterian Church	*"Many teenagers experience same sex attractions. For most these do not linger but are part of their sexual development. For others their sexual development can be arrested by various factors in their upbringing including close family relationships and family breakdown. In our culture, that includes the promotion of alternative sexualities, this can result in some young people being confused about their sexuality. They may need help to understand and work through deeper-seated insecurities, issues of forgiveness, gender acceptance and self-acceptance before they can come to terms with their sexual identity."* Pastoral Guidelines – Homosexuality, Social Issues and Resources Panel

FOR YOUR FOLDER

Make a brief summary of the views of the Catholic, Anglican and Presbyterian Churches.

IN A GROUP

1. Explain why the issue of homosexuality causes controversy for the Christian Church.

2. Do you imagine that there will ever be a change of attitude regarding homosexuality among the leadership of these churches?

FURTHER THINKING

What Bible texts shape the Churches' views on homosexuality?

CLASS DEBATE

"The teachings of the Bible do not change, so the attitude of the churches to moral issues should not change."

Do you agree or disagree? Give reasons for your answer.

FURTHER THINKING

Divide into groups of four.

Choose one of the following topics to research:

- The age of consent
- Alcohol and drug use
- Christian involvement in politics
- Same-sex marriage blessings
- Attitudes to war
- Responsibility towards the environment
- Treatment for infertility

Find out what the different Christian denominations have to say about the issue.

Use the internet or interview your local priest or minister.

FOR YOUR FOLDER

1. Describe the work of one organisation which helps bring together Christians from different traditions.

2. Why do many Christians think that it is important to understand the beliefs and values of traditions different from their own?

3. Do you think the Christian Church has the right to speak out about changing moral standards in our society? Give reasons for your answer, showing that you have considered more than one point of view.

Index

Acknowledgements

Authors' acknowledgements

Many thanks to Sheila Johnston, recently retired from Colourpoint Books and to Donna Finlay from CCEA for the opportunity to work on this book, and to Michael Spence and Rachel Irwin at Colourpoint. Particular thanks to the SVP Conference at Our Lady and St Patrick's College, Belfast; to Dominic Kealey and Angela Killen; to Laura Mullan, Debbie Cunningham and Bronagh Rice for allowing me to shadow them on their visitation work; and to Mrs A O'Rahilly and family, for their generous and gracious welcome into their home. Thank you to Stephen and Claire McCaffrey for the insights they shared and thanks also to Maeve Byrne, Rachel McCloskey and Hannah McGrath for sharing their experiences of the Community Service work carried out by the students of Our Lady and St Patrick's College, Belfast.

A special thank you to Gerry, Rónán, Éile and Tiarnán for their support and patience.

Anne Hughes

A special thanks to Sheila Johnston, Michael Spence and Rachel Irwin from Colourpoint Books for their professional guidance and support; and to Donna Finlay from CCEA for the opportunity to work on this book; thanks also to Rev Steve Stockman, Canon Walter Lewis and the Rev Ken Newell for their expertise; thanks to Rachel Gardiner for her personal contribution. Thanks to all the churches that gave kind permission for photographs to be used.

A special thank you to Martin, Tom and Kate for their encouragement and support.

Juliana Gilbride